Economic Decision Making

PRIVATE AND PUBLIC DECISIONS

Economic
Decision
Making

PRIVATE AND PUBLIC DECISIONS

edited by SISAY ASEFA, *Western Michigan University*

89-248

IOWA STATE UNIVERSITY PRESS / *Ames, Iowa*

Printed by The Iowa State University Press, Ames, Iowa 50010

First edition, 1985

Library of Congress Cataloging in Publication Data
Main entry under title:

Economic decision making.

"Six essays adapted from the presentations made during the seventeenth annual Economics Department Seminar-Lecture series at Western Michigan University" — Pref.
Includes index.
1. Economic policy — Decision making — Addresses, essays, lectures. I. Sisay, Asefa, 1950-   . II. Western Michigan University. Dept. of Economics.
HD87.E25   1985   338.9   84-25162
ISBN 0-8138-0111-7

The text in this book was printed from camera-ready copy provided by the editor.

CONTENTS

PREFACE

This book contains six essays adapted from the presentations made during the seventeenth annual Economics Department Seminar-Lecture Series at Western Michigan University. The theme of the series, which took place during the academic year 1982-1983, was "Applied Economics: Private and Public Decisions."

Applied economics is viewed as a body of knowledge that comprises applications of economic analysis and method to decision making of private and public economic institutions. The objective of each author was to explore applied economics in its various dimensions and to show the relevance of economic analysis to either private economic decision making or to an area of public policy.

The essays in this book are concerned with applications of economic analysis to crucial economic issues in higher education, health care, corporations, agriculture, economic growth and development, and the environment.

In the preparation of this book, I am indebted to the participants in the Seminar-Lecture Series for their cooperation. I wish to thank members of the Economics Department of Western Michigan University, especially professors Werner Sichel and Raymond Zelder, for their enthusiastic support during my efforts in organizing and directing this series. I would like to thank the Dean of the College of Arts and Sciences and the Department of Economics for jointly sponsoring the Seminar-Lecture Series. Particular thanks should be extended to the members of the lectures committee for the 1982-1983 academic year, Professors Myron Ross and Bassam Harik. My thanks also go to the Economics Department secretaries, Becky Ryder and Bonnie Guminski, for their excellent clerical services.

Finally, I sincerely thank the members of my family, my
wife, Wegayehu (Mimi), my daughter, Aden, and my son,
Beniam, for their patience and understanding during the
long hours I spent with the lecture series and the preparation of this book rather than with them.

INTRODUCTION

James Koch discusses the relationship between economics and academic administration. He raises two central
questions in his essay: whether there is a distinctly
economic way of thinking about and meeting the challenges
and problems of academic administration and whether this
economic approach is more attractive than other available
approaches to academic decision making.

Koch contends that economic analysis does not provide
a set of selected answers and conclusions but instead of-
fers a tool kit and method of approaching academic decisions, such as a recognition of alternatives and choices
and an emphasis on substitutions and trade-offs to achieve
given objectives. He calls for using the concept of opportunity cost, stressing the point that most services
provided by universities are not free and the appropriate
pricing of these facilities should eliminate inefficien-
cies in their use. He points out that the use of marginal
analysis, in which the additional benefits of each decision alternative are weighed against the costs, can be a
powerful tool in academic decision making.

Koch concludes that most of the necessary and useful
economic concepts applicable to academic administration
can be learned from a good introductory economic theory
course.

Paul Feldstein is concerned with the economics of
health and medical care. He addresses two related questions: whether the health care sector is likely to expand
in the future and whether hospitals are insulated from the
economic and demographic factors that affect the growth,
maturity, and eventual decline of other industries. He

discusses such factors as the determinants of hospital
revenues and costs, the changing nature of hospital markets, and the economic choices facing hospitals and the
rest of the health care sector.

     According to Feldstein, population growth has a major
impact on hospital revenues. He contends that the use of
hospitals and other health care facilities by the aged
(over 65) has been increasing in recent years. Hospital
revenues from the aged are very much affected by government policy, especially the attempt to hold down expenditures on medicare and medicaid programs. Private providers
(e.g., insurance companies) are also attempting to lower
hospital costs. The effect of these policies will be to
limit the growth of hospital revenues.

     Feldstein argues that health care and hospital costs,
however, will continue to rise due to: (1) advances in
medical technology that may increase the cost of medical
equipment, (2) the declining percentage of younger age
population that may result in a smaller supply of nurses
and result in higher wages for them, and (3) the phasing
out of government subsidies for capital and health manpower.

     Feldstein discusses the changing markets for hospi-
tals and health care. He points out that the larger supply of physicians will compete with hospitals by performing hospital services in their own offices. A higher
level of concentration will occur in the hospital sector
to realize potential economies of scale from affiliations
with other hospitals.

     Feldstein notes that in the 1960s and 1970s the de-
mand for health care was high and hospitals were generously reimbursed on a cost-plus basis. Hospitals in the
1980s, on the other hand, will be pressured to adjust to
declining revenues and demand, especially in the Northeast
and the Midwest.

     Feldstein concludes that as hospitals face limited
increases in revenues, rising costs, and increased competition, they must make difficult choices, such as hospital
merger into large health care and multihospital systems,
seeking protection through legislation, and diversification.

     Alvin Karchere argues that the standard theory of the
firm is more useful in making normative decisions than in
describing the behavior of businesses. Even in the normative sense, he notes, the usefulness of economic theory is

somewhat limited because most important business problems
are concerned with innovation in manufacturing, management, or product development, rather than with optimization of known demand and production functions. He dis-
agrees with John Kenneth Galbraith's view that corporations do not operate within the market system, instead
controlling the economy through planning mechanisms. He
agrees with Herbert Simon's and Gunnar Eliasson's notion
that corporations are satisficers rather than optimizers.
He considers Baumol's theory of contestable markets to be
useful in defending and modifying the standard theory of
the firm. According to Baumol, a situation similar to perfect competition exists in a contestable market because of
the threat of entry by potential competitors.

Karchere, while considering the concept of the contestable market a useful idea that needs further research,
points out that Baumol's assumptions are as unrealistic as
the assumptions of the original standard theory. He sug-
gests that the application of the contestable market concept to international trade, which implies trade barrier
removal that increases potential competitors and thus enhances economic welfare by creating greater efficiency and
innovation, adds very little to the conclusion reached by
traditional international trade theory.

Earl Heady deals with the potentials and restraints
of world food production, pointing out that as long as the
world experiences oscillating transitory patterns and food
cycles, sustained long-run solutions are unlikely.

In his assessment of world food production restraints, potentials, and policies, Heady evaluates six
sources of increasing world food production: (1) increasing yield through improved technologies; (2) intensive use of currently cultivated land through multiple
cropping and other related methods of efficient utilization of available rainfall and solar energy; (3) bringing
uncultivated land into production; (4) preventing against
crop losses to rodents, birds, and spoilage; (5) diverting
greater proportions of grain from livestock consumption to
human consumption; and (6) producing more food from sea
and ocean resources.

The diverting of world grain production from livestock to human consumption is difficult and controversial,
according to Heady. It implies shifting grain consumption
from rich countries, where per capita consumption of grain
through meat is high, to poorer countries, where it is

low. The most promising source of increasing food production in developing countries is through land already cultivated. If developing countries could raise their land
productivity to the level of developed countries, world
food production could be increased by 67 percent.

Heady contends that many developing countries, although threatened with future food shortages, tend to
adopt policies that undervalue agriculture. This is reflected in policies that depress prices to farmers in
order to reduce retail food prices for urban consumption
and that keep input prices high and impose taxes on farm
exports. He argues that policies of some developed countries also have adverse effects on agricultural productivity of developing countries, such as the United States'
P.L. 480 program.

According to Heady, realization of potential sources
of food production, which depends on removing restraints,
does not involve new and mysterious processes but rather
the effective execution of processes already known and
practiced in agricultural research and a conducive administrative and political climate in developing countries.

Heady warns that producing enough food to keep up
with population growth, as well as eliminating existing
global malnutrition, over the next thirty years will not
solve the even longer run problems of population growth
over the next hundred years. The means of dealing with
this controversial issue must include, in addition to current educational and technical birth control methods, increased per capita income, adequate social security or
old-age pension programs, and the further improvement in
the education, employment, and socioeconomic participation
of women.

Heady is cautiously optimistic about future world
food production. He considers the socioeconomic policy
restraints to be more crucial than the physical restraints
and believes that in order to increase world food production over the next thirty or forty years it will be necessary for developing countries to remove all policy restraints that depress incentives to use more purchased
farm inputs, that interfere with trade, or that discourage
investment in agricultural resources and personnel.

Robert Dorfman addresses the underlying ethical standards of environmental laws and their effect on the national effort to protect and improve the environment. He
contends that indecisiveness and confusion in implementing

environmental laws originate from two contradictory standards that the government is trying to work under simultaneously, the natural rights doctrine and the principle of
utilitarianism. The essence of the doctrine of natural
rights is that every person has certain inherent and inviolable rights (e.g., life, health, sanctity of property)
that cannot be legitimately invaded by the government for
the benefit of others. The principle of utilitarianism
implies that it is the right of the government to take
action to increase the public welfare.

The inviolable natural rights are the rationale for
environmental regulations (e.g., the Clean Water Act),
which protect an individual's life, health, and private
property from contamination by pollutants and other tox-
ins. Utilitarianism, however, is clearly implied by the
benefit-cost goals of the Water Resources Act.

Dorfman argues that most legislators believe in both
principles, to varying degrees. Therefore, government
regulations in general and environmental laws in particular are written to implement contradictory ethical principles. He presents three examples of environmental legislation that illustrate the problems that arise: the
Clean Water Act, the Clean Air Act, and the Toxic Substances Control Act. Dorfman argues that benefit-cost
analysis alone is insufficient to resolve the conflicts
in the principles, because monetary values cannot be
placed on natural rights.

Borrowing a concept from philosopher John Rowls who
classifies social goals into primary and secondary values
depending on whether they concern natural rights or the
public welfare, Dorfman proposes a decision-making approach for the EPA. He would like to see the agency perform standard benefit-cost analyses by keeping track of
the extent to which natural rights are invaded and then
judge whether the superior economic choice is advantageous
enough to justify any infringement on individual rights.

Arnold Harberger begins with three general points:
(1) economic science can be useful in various kinds of
political environments and ideologies; (2) trade-offs occur when people give up economic goals in order to achieve
political and social ones; and (3) policymakers may be
forced to accept inferior economic solutions because of
political realities.

The remainder of Harberger's essay is devoted to an
application of economic analysis to the economic growth of

developing countries. He notes that development economics
in the 1950s was heavily influenced by the Harrod-Domar
models and "surplus labor" theories that placed physical
capital as the only constraint factor to economic growth.
The result was an outgrowth of misguided policies with
little relevance to the economic realities of most developing countries. He believes that modern development
economics recognizes the complexity of the growth process
and does not succumb to the naive oversimplifications of
the 1950s. Among the factors that influenced this new
view of economic growth, according to Harberger, are the
modern theory of economic growth and the theory of effective protection, which call for the liberalization of
trade and the equalization of tariff rates.

The modern theory of economic growth, Harberger contends, is an application of the neoclassical theory of
marginal productivity, in which the national income growth
is divided into contributions of labor, capital, and a
residual factor.

Harberger points out that development economists
have gained experience and learned some modest lessons,
such as the limitations inherent in large macroeconomic,
input-output, and sectoral planning models; the limitations in using taxation as a means of improving income
distribution; the fact that fulfilling basic needs may be
more reliable than income distribution as a guide to economic policy; and the fact that under certain circumstances potential efficiency can be gained from public
enterprises. When comparing recent successes and failures
in many developing countries, he finds that the successful
countries consider the economic growth policy decision to
be a technical problem of doing the right thing, while the
unsuccessful countries tend to be entangled in political
and ideological problems.

Harberger argues that a sound economic policy is one
that leads private decision makers in the direction of
socially desirable action, while recognizing the complexity of the growth process. This may be accomplished by
making private benefits and costs as close as possible to
social benefits and costs and by using government policy
to offset negative private externalities. He stresses the
importance of human capital formation as one of the best
prescriptions for the long-run economic growth of developing countries.

Economic Decision Making

PRIVATE AND PUBLIC DECISIONS

1 *The Economist and Academic Administration*

JAMES V. KOCH

The relevance of economic analysis to the administration of higher education has always been a matter of some dispute. In the eyes of many academics, the field of economics has dealt with the baser and less attractive aspects of human existence. The oft-quoted judgment of Carlyle that economics is the dismal science continues to hold sway in many academic precincts. By inference, economists themselves have often been considered to be proponents of a secular Philistinic religion antithetical to the humanistic ideals that underpin a liberal education. The lament of Edmund Burke that the age of the "sophister, economists, and calculator" has dawned still has currency in much of the professoriate (Samuelson 1973, 1).

The typical academic notes that the profit-maximizing assumption underpinning many economic models is substantially inappropriate to the world of higher education. Also, most academics have greeted with hostility the introduction of modern management techniques often associated with economists (for example, zero-based budgeting). Further, as scientific philosophers some economists are logical positivists who, when their attitudes are especially hardened, aver, "If you can't measure it, it's not worth knowing about" or even "If you can't measure it, it doesn't exist." Such philosophic positions, when combined with the propensity of some modern economists to engage in highly abstract and quantitative analyses, have led to skepticism in the academy about whether economists have any special competencies to contribute to academic administration. As a consequence, economists have often been banished to the most remote rooms of the academic house, to be summoned to academic administration posts only when

3

they are perceived either to ignore or to reject the reputed postulates of their academic discipline.

Two questions will be raised in this chapter: Is there a distinctively economic way of thinking about, and meeting, the problems and challenges of academic administration? and Is the economic approach to academic administration more or less effective than other approaches that are available? To answer these questions we must establish what economics is all about, hastening our progress in that direction by specifying what economics is <u>not</u>.

A TOOL KIT, NOT A SET OF PROBLEMS AND SOLUTIONS

While there are many different views concerning what the field of economics is all about, an increasingly popular view is that the study of economics is designed to furnish a way of analyzing and thinking about choice situations so that intelligent decisions can be made. The study of economics is not designed to produce a canned set of answers concerning what decision makers should do, or a list of policies, which if pursued by a university president will always lead to good results. It is of course true that economists, fledgling and otherwise, generally hold opinions about which economic policies should be followed in certain circumstances. However, as Keynes once noted, "Economics does not furnish a body of settled conclusions....It is a method, rather than a doctrine, an application of the mind, a technique of thinking which helps its possessor to draw correct conclusions" (McKenzie and Tullock 1978, 500).

The manner in which economists think about making choices, the assumptions that they make in so doing, the models that they utilize to generate explanations and predictions, these are the tools in an economist's kit. It is this kit of tools, and not specific subject matter, that seemingly differentiates the economist-administrator from other administrators. For example, it is apparent that many fields of study examine issues such as the appropriate level of tuition to charge students or the effects of released time on research productivity. Economist-administrators are not distinguishable from other administrators on the basis of the issues confronted and examined; rather, they are arguably unique in the way that they approach and solve these problems. (We must bear in mind that neither knowledge as a whole nor academic

disciplines in particular are so rigidly compartmentalized
that we can realistically state that the attitudes and
approaches we attribute to economists are not sometimes
characteristic of other academic disciplines. But just as
surely as we live in an intellectual age of multidiscipli-
nary endeavors and borrowing of knowledge across disciplinary lines, so also we operate in a milieu in which disciplinary specialists are in fact trained rather narrowly
and often rigidly in their graduate programs. For example, very few Ph.D. degree programs in economics involve
more than a smattering of course work in fields other than
economics. Hence, a specific academic discipline acquires
logics, attitudes, rites, and even people peculiar to the
confines of that discipline. This helps us explain why
the "tribe" we call economists is reasonably separate and
distinct in terms of its attitudes and approaches to problems.)

DISTINCTIVE ECONOMIC ATTITUDES AND THEIR EFFECTS ON ADMINISTRATION

The following five different attitudes and approaches, which are characteristic of economics, can
result in a differentiated style of academic administration.

Alternatives: There Nearly Always Are More Than We Think

Economic analysis stresses that in almost any situation there are a variety of ways to accomplish a specific
goal. The task of the economist is to identify those alternatives and then to assess accurately the costs and
benefits associated with each. What the economist does is
to construct what might be considered a menu, complete
with pictures and prices. Customers (decision makers) can
then choose what they wish to purchase.

Academics (the author included) are often guilty of
ignoring or failing to consider relevant alternatives.
Consider the faculty member who desires a salary increment
higher than the 5 percent provided by the state legisla-
ture. He or she typically regards as retrograde and unthinkable any suggestions that a larger salary increment
of, say, 10 percent, might be generated by decreasing the
size of the faculty. Many faculty members talk with a
disapproving air about suggestions of this sort, which
they view as requiring the "cannibalization" of worthy
colleagues. Yet; the mean student/faculty ratio in

public institutions has in fact been rising in recent
years (according to the ratios reported in the annual
faculty salary surveys of the American Association of University Professors). This unthinkable option is in actu-
ality being exercised to some degree in public higher education, for example, in the state of Michigan. The economist, while not necessarily approving of this trend,
would point it out and include it in any discussion of
choices available.

Or consider the faculty member who toils at a private
college and who recoils in anger in response to suggestions that Ivy University might reduce its financial problems by admitting more students. Certainly the admission
of more students would bring with it a range of new problems; however, it would also generally increase Ivy University's revenues. Once again, the unthinkable is in
fact being undertaken by some private colleges and universities.

The moral is that in most academic situations that
require decisions to be made there are usually more
choices available than are immediately apparent. Academic
administrators must avoid becoming fixated on specific
segments of complex decision problems. For example, an
institution's tuition and fee policy is clearly an important influence on both enrollment and academic quality.
But so also are the decisions that the institution makes
(often by default) with respect to admissions, retention,
and exit standards; housing; extracurricular and other
nonacademic programs; and the range and diversity of academic programs. In fact a multitude of ways exists to
differentiate, position, and improve a college or university in the heterogeneous market of higher education
(Kotler 1975; Mayhew 1979; Grabowski 1981). The key initially is for the academic administrator to see the entire
decision picture and subsequently to understand the trade-
offs and substitutions implied in each alternative.

Identifying and clarifying choices are familiar exercises to economists, for their theoretical models often
assume the smooth substitutability of one input for another and the ultimate selection by a decision maker of an
optimal strategy from among the available choices. To be
sure, the world is seldom as simple as it appears in economic textbooks. Nonetheless, it is arguably true that
the option unthinkable (or perhaps unrecognized) to some
administrators is just another evaluated option in most
economic models. While economic logic as such does not

endorse per se strategies such as decreasing the size of
faculty or lowering academic standards, these are available options and economic logic demands, in effect, "let's
take a look."

Substitutions and Trade-Offs

Because economic models stress the substitutability
of one thing for another, there is considerable emphasis
in economics on determining what the trade-off is when one
product (for example, instructions by a graduate assistant) is substituted for another product (lectures given
by a professor). The trade-off is often viewed in terms
of some third variable that represents what is being at-
tempted to be produced or accomplished. In the case at
hand, it might be the mean student performance on an examination. How many additional graduate assistants must be
added in order to make up the loss of one lecture per week
by the professor? The answer is a trade-off ratio, or
rate of substitution.

Suppose we determine that two student sessions with a
graduate assistant will generate learning benefits equivalent to one lecture by the professor. What will that
tell us? It could suggest that we ought to employ more
graduate assistants. Why? Suppose each graduate assistant is paid $5,000 per year, while the professor is paid
$25,000 per year. It does not take a mathematician to see
that we can produce a given amount of learning less expen-
sively by employing more graduate assistants and fewer
professors. Heresy, you say? No, it is not heresy; rather it is one of the choices that many colleges and universities have increasingly been making in recent years.

Academic administrators are charged, among other
things, with doing the best possible job with the limited
resources at their disposal. The public, the trustees,
and even faculty and students reasonably demand that academic administrators attempt to maximize the welfare of
the institution (however conceived), given the resources
at hand. But the only way administrators can do this is
by determining and applying such trade-offs. Trade-offs
are especially critical, and especially visible, when the
basic teaching-learning process is involved. Should a
class be taught by graduate assistants, instructors, full
professors, or television? Does computer-assisted instruction (CAI) enhance student academic performance, or
would scarce monies be better devoted to making classes
smaller in size? How many class sections should be

sacrificed to generate a faculty-authored book published by a reputable university press?

The above list of questions illustrates the large number of trade-offs that academic administrators must make on an everyday basis. In each case there is more than one way to accomplish a given end; the intelligent administrator substitutes one input for another in order to accomplish a given goal at the least possible cost. This strategy frees the maximum amount of money for other tasks, be they heating buildings, supporting faculty research, or fielding winning football teams.

But trade-offs sometimes lead to results that at first seem to be counterintuitive or even nonsensical. Consider the role of CAI instruction on student performance in the classroom. CAI has the potential to increase student performance in a particular class, but will it? The answer depends on a complex set of substitutions and trade-offs. Suppose John is taking a beginning sociology course and is offered the option of undertaking learning activity by means of CAI. If John utilizes CAI and if it is efficient as a teaching-learning tool relative to other teaching-learning methods (for example, reading the textbook), then John's performance on sociology examinations should rise. His performance in sociology may not rise at all, however, if John finds that he no longer needs to study sociology as much in order to achieve a given score on the sociology examination. He may, in fact, decrease the total number of study hours devoted to sociology (including CAI time) and instead spend the additional free hours sleeping, working, or studying for other courses.

The net effect of a more efficient method of teaching sociology, therefore, may ironically be no increase at all in student performance on sociology examinations. Instead, the students' scores on examinations in other courses may rise and they may sleep more, work more, or otherwise distribute the newly free hours. Indeed it can come to pass that a very skilled and very efficient instructor of sociology might perforce cause students to study sociology less and other subjects more. The economist-administrator knows that this result not only is quite possible but also is completely within the realm of economic possibilities (Chizmar et al. 1977).

Of course, students are not the only ones who behave in the fashion just described. Faculty, administrators, and staff also have incentives to substitute one thing for another. For example, will reducing the teaching load

cause professors so favored to spend more time teaching
and preparing for the reduced number of classes? Possibly. But both economic theory and experience suggest that
the professors may well spend more time on research, public service, consulting, or coffee breaks. Teaching and
preparation time per class might actually decrease. Or
consider the introduction of a labor-saving device such as
a word processor. Will this cause the office that in-
stalls one to do more work? It could. But it could also
result in the same work being done more easily, and longer
coffee breaks. Hence any administrator must be careful,
or at the very least, knowledgeable, when proposing new
and more efficient ways of doing things. Substitutions
inspired by such "efficient" innovations may be complex
and, in some cases, even counterintuitive.

A final word on trade-offs and substitutions. Wise
administrators will attempt to identify the actual trade-
offs that they face whenever possible. Only in a minority
of cases will they be able to assign numeric values to
these trade-offs. But they must have some notion about
the approximate size and direction of the trade-offs in
order to function intelligently. Only then will they begin to be able to assess with accuracy what the institution sacrifices when it makes a particular choice. That
brings us to our next consideration.

Opportunity Costs and Zero Prices

One of the most distinctive economic doctrines is
that of an opportunity cost. The opportunity cost of an
action is the most valuable foregone alternative that is
given up because that action has been taken. For example,
the opportunity cost of a student's attending college is
perceived by the student to be at least as great as what
that student could have earned had he or she chosen instead to remain at home and work full-time. An economist
computing the cost (that is, opportunity cost) of a student attending college includes not only the directly observable costs of tuition, fees, books, and so forth, but
also the foregone income the student could have earned
but does not because of college attendance. Thus if
tuition and fees and related expenses approximate $2,000
per year at a public institution and the student could
have earned a net of $8,000 working full-time instead,
the total economic cost to the student of the college education is $10,000. (Note that room and board has not been
included as a cost. This reflects the fact that the

student would have incurred room and board costs in any
case even if not attending college, so they are not ex-
plicitly attributable to college attendance.)

   The economist-administrator who thinks in terms of
opportunity costs will not be mystified, as some administrators were, by the apparently unexpected increase in
college enrollments in fall of 1980 (Fall enrollment
1980). Some administrators had argued that rising tuition
rates and a declining number of high school graduates
would put a serious dent in enrollments. Instead quite
the opposite happened. Why? Because both teenage and
general rates of unemployment were high and rising higher.
A student who attends college does not forfeit $8,000 in
income if he or she would not have had a job anyway; one
cannot lose what one has never had. Therefore for many
individuals the opportunity cost (an economist would say
the actual economic cost) of attending college fell in
1980 because of the tepid state of the economy and the
high rate of unemployment. This reduction in the cost of
attending college caused more individuals to attend
college, a logical and predictable result, if one is
thinking in terms of the opportunity cost concept.

   Another area of academe where grievous allocation
errors are made because of ignorance of the opportunity
cost concept is the input or service provided by the academic institution to faculty and others "free" or at a
very low price, such as university automobiles, computer
services, electricity, telephone service, and media services. Telephone service provides an example. Assume
that the Department of Physics can make whatever telephone
calls it wishes, including long distance calls, with the
costs of these calls absorbed by the university budget and
no charge levied against the department. Now these telephone calls are not truly free, since the university must
pay for them. But the Department of Physics, which does
not have to pay for them, tends to use the telephone far
more than it would if it had to pay for the calls from de-
partmental funds.

   For a university as a whole, then, the opportunity
cost of a long distance telephone call is whatever the
university could have purchased with the money that it
must pay to the telephone company because the call has
been made. The opportunity cost might be stated in terms
of library books not purchased, or research grants not
funded, or whatever, and is quite simply the most valuable
of all of these things that has been sacrificed because of

the call. The lesson here is that "There's no such thing
as a free lunch." Somebody must sacrifice and give up
something because of the telephoning done by the Department of Physics. In this case, it is the university.
Somebody always pays--if not with money, then with the
sacrifice of other attractive possible uses of resources.
That is the essence of the opportunity cost concept, and
it is an idea that has obvious applicability to academic
administration. Effective academic administrators must
sooner or later think and act in terms of the opportunity
cost concept. The administrator who does not recognize
that every decision requires the sacrifice of attractive
alternatives is destined to have recurring problems.

The Role of Prices

The Department of Physics telephone usage problem
occurred because no penalty was assessed on the department
for such usage; that is, the price of the telephone usage
was zero. When, as in this case, the individuals who use
a university resource are not the same individuals who pay
for that resource, problems and distortions often arise.
Consider the case of automobile usage, which on many cam-
puses is not charged back to users; if an automobile trip
is "university business," and an automobile is available,
the driver may use the car without charge. These services
are typically overused (overused here meaning that there
is substantially more demand for the use of these resources than there would be if the users of these resources had to pay for them). Consequently, undesirable
situations arise. First, given that the number of available university automobiles is fixed, prospective users
often find that all automobiles have already been booked
(a classic case of excess demand at an existing price).
Second, the scarce automobiles end up allocated to users
who requested them first, those at the head of the queue.
The relative importance or centrality of the business for
which they are necessary is ignored.

Some academic institutions react to these two undesirable conditions by establishing priorities. A priority
"A" request receives an automobile in preference to a priority "B" request, and so forth. Such an allocational
system improves a bad situation but does not eliminate
frivolous use of automobiles. The priority system also
does not force priority "A" drivers to recognize the fact
that their use of the automobile imposes a cost on the
university. Finally, the operation of such a system can

be complicated. For example, can an "A" priority driver
bump a "B" priority driver and, if so, on how much notice?

Most of the above problems would be eliminated if the
university adopted a pricing system for scarce resources,
such as automobiles and computer services. (If the resources are not scarce, it is a sign that the university
has too many of them.) The price of the resource per unit
should reflect two things: (1) the additional cost to the
university of supplying that resource unit to the user and
(2) the demand for these particular resource units. High-
cost, high-demand resources will therefore have higher
prices attached to them. In the language of the previous
section, users pay what amounts to the opportunity cost
that they have imposed on the university by their use of
that resource.

The prices are designed to achieve a more efficient
and judicious use of scarce university resources. Prices
force consumer-users of resources to choose consciously
how they will spend their limited budgets and to confront
the real trade-offs that exist in any university situation. Despite the emotional and sometimes ideological
opposition that some academics have to pricing the inputs
and outputs of higher education, such pricing can help a
university lower bloated telephone bills, avoid out-of-
control automobile and photocopier usage, discourage frivolous use of physical plant personnel, and reduce queues
at the computer center at the most popular times of the
day (Skolnick 1980; Hoenack 1982).

Pricing academic resources and relying on the logic
of a pricing system to solve many allocational problems is
one of the distinctive characteristics of the economic
approach to academic administration. Hence an economist-
administrator instinctively leans toward pricing as a
means of allocating many academic resources. When an
economist-administrator avoids pricing a resource, it
is ordinarily for one of two reasons: either the cost of
instituting and operating a pricing system would exceed
the benefits of the system or there is a well-developed
rationale for individuals and departments to use more of a
resource than they would if they had to pay a price equal
to the opportunity cost associated with that use. Library
resources on occasion are an example of this latter cir-
cumstance, although even a tyro administrator soon becomes
aware of the penchant of some departments to make profli-
gate journal and book purchases unless otherwise con-
strained. Patronage of the university's symphony orches-
tra and even attendance at its football games are, some

would argue, further examples of cases in which scarce resources cannot be priced by the opportunity cost principle, without eliciting undesirable results. In the jargon of the economist, these cases (library, symphony, football team) are allegedly "external economies" and therefore ordinary pricing is inappropriate unless accompanied by specific subsidies. (In such circumstances, the private marginal cost of an action is perceived to be more than the social marginal cost, the latter being the appropriate guide to efficient resource usage. Thus it is thought to be appropriate to subsidize the activity or to alter its price in order to overcome the problem. This argument, of course, underpins the subsidization and low tuition that characterize public institutions of higher education.)

Marginal Costs, Average Costs, and the Economic Way of Thinking

Economists are apt to talk in terms of marginal concepts, such as marginal cost and marginal revenue. Marginal cost in this context is the additional cost incurred because of the production of one additional unit of output. Thus the marginal cost of admitting one additional student to State Tech is whatever could have been accomplished with the additional or incremental resources that must be sacrificed in order to accommodate that student. It is apparent that in some cases the marginal cost of admitting an additional student to a program is zero, or close to zero, because no new instructors or resources must be devoted to handling that student; quite the reverse is true in other cases.

Most individuals, and most academic administrators, however, are more accustomed to thinking in terms of average cost concepts. Administrators usually have some idea about the average cost concept such as the average cost of educating one of their students or the average cost per credit hour of instruction in the various areas of their jurisdiction. The average costs that they have in mind can be illustrated with a simple example. Suppose that the only cost of offering an English composition class is the wage paid to the professor. If the professor's salary is $24,000 and he or she teaches six courses during the academic year, a typical university will charge $4,000 ($24,000/6) of that professor's salary to each English composition class. With twenty students in the class, the average cost per student is $200 ($4,000/20).

Similar average cost computations can be made for any academic course, for academic departments, and for entire

universities. These cost computations typically ignore
the use of nonpriced resources, such as scarce classroom
space, heat, and light, but usually are reasonable approximations of the average personnel costs of educating a
typical student.

Armed with average cost data, an academic administrator can make some inferences about programs that are costly in an overall sense; however, that same administrator
typically cannot use the same average cost data to make
inferences about what it would cost to educate additional
students. Therein lies the rub. Consider the actual case
of the president of a prestigious private university that,
during the 1970s, was faced with severe financial problems. At a faculty meeting at that university, a faculty
member suggested that one possible cure for the institution's financial bind was to admit more students. Since
at that time the mean tuition charge per student at the
university approximated $4,000 annually, and the univer-
sity had many more qualified applicants than it chose to
admit, the faculty member reasoned that the admission of
perhaps 100 additional students would generate an incremental $400,000 annually and solve the short-run problem.

But the president of the institution demurred. Not-
ing that the average cost of educating a student at the
university was in the neighborhood of $7,000, he argued
that the university would lose $3,000 ($7,000 - $4,000)
per additional student. The faculty member's suggestion,
he asserted, was an excellent recipe for bankruptcy.

In fact, however, the marginal cost of admitting an
additional student to the university was reasonably close
to zero. Empty spaces existed in most university class-
rooms and in university housing. Perhaps no more than
$50,000 would have been needed to employ additional fac-
ulty and support services because of the additional 100
students. Therefore, if quality considerations did not
dictate otherwise, the faculty member's recommendation
that additional students be admitted would have garnered
the university a potential net gain of $350,000.

The faculty member's analysis relied on marginal cost
data, while the president's analysis relied on average
cost data. The faculty member's analysis was easily the
more relevant and cogent in this case. The university
could in fact have improved its financial position by admitting more students even though in an average cost sense
it was losing money with the admission of every additional
student. The point is that, in this situation, marginal

cost as a concept was much more useful than average cost;
the university would not incur that average cost per
student when it admitted an additional student.
The university had only to bear the marginal cost per
student, represented roughly by the $50,000 divided
by the 100 additional students, or only about $500 per
student. It was this point the president missed.

The distinction between marginal cost and average
cost and, for that matter, the reliance that economists
place on marginal concepts in general, are central to the
thinking of any economist-administrators worth their salt.
The economist-administrator constantly focuses on the
costs and benefits of moving from one situation to another
and devotes less attention to the costs already incurred
that have resulted in the current situation. What is to
be gained from employing, for example, additional baseball
coaches? The first coach hired may make a significant
contribution to the team's performance, and a second may
also achieve good things. But a third, a fourth, and a
fifth assistant baseball coach? At some point, the marginal contribution of an additional assistant baseball
coach is likely to be slight even though the team as a
whole wins nearly every game. The mean number of baseball
wins per coach may be large even while the contribution of
the last assistant baseball coach hired is negligible.
This is what the famous Law of Diminishing Returns warns.
But note that the Law of Diminishing Returns, and the
moral of this story, depends on thinking in marginal or
incremental terms rather than in terms of averages or
means.

Economist-administrators who think in marginal terms
are likely to question on purely economic grounds the
worth of undergraduate majors and specializations that require an excessive number of credit hours. They are vi-
tally interested in knowing whether it is more productive
to split six hours of faculty research time between two
faculty members or instead to assign the entire six hours
to a single faculty member. They are critically aware
that average faculty salary data usually disguise much and
often provide precious little information about the relevant marginal salary cost associated with hiring, for example, a computer scientist or an electrical engineer as a
new faculty member.

George Stigler, always a sage observer of human
events, has aptly summarized the economic way of thinking
(and the marginal decision calculus that it implies) in a

classic statement that has surprisingly general applicability to human behavior and special relevance to decision
making in higher education: "Ignorance is like subzero
weather; by a sufficient expenditure its effects upon
people can be kept within tolerable or even comfortable
bounds, but it would be wholly uneconomic entirely to
eliminate all its effects" (Stigler 1961).

The astute economist-administrator takes Stigler's
advice to heart. There exists a veritable legion of good
things on which to spend a university's money—library
books, faculty travel, summer research, scholarships. But
building the best library in all of academe may require
that a university spend nothing on faculty travel, summer
research, and student scholarships. Indeed, for many
universities it may require eliminating faculty salaries.
Clearly having the best library, or even a superior library, is a very good thing but probably (most would
agree) not worth the sacrifice. Similarly, faculty research is a worthwhile goal (a "good" in the lexicon of
the economist) but probably not so worthwhile as to sacrifice everything else to accomplish it.

The crucial question for an academic administrator,
then, is not whether something such as faculty travel is
good but rather how good, and what are the alternative
uses for the same resources? Just as it would be entirely
uneconomic to attempt to eliminate all germs or to eliminate all automobile fatalities, it is ordinarily uneconomic to emphasize faculty travel to the total disregard of
library books, or vice versa.

Marginal decision making implies carefully weighing
the additional benefits and costs associated with each option available. The polar opposite of marginal decision
making is the all-too-common administrative practice of
increasing every unit's budget by the same percent or giving all faculty the same salary raise, regardless of performance and circumstances. Administrators who consistently do this may avoid controversy but will only by ac-
cident make the best possible use of the scarce resources
that they command. "Across the boardism" is often a sign
that administrators have forfeited their responsibilities.
Excellence, whether defined by the economist or the noneconomist, is seldom consonant with treating all units the
same.

THE MATTER OF QUANTIFICATION

Since the late 1950s economists have routinely been

required to master large doses of mathematics and statistics as a part of their graduate school training. In the
better graduate schools and in the major journals of the
discipline it is often the case that equations are only
occasionally interrupted with words. There are tales,
perhaps apocryphal, of practicing economists with verbal
skills so minimal that they communicate only by means of
computer printouts. The specter of an incommunicative,
number-crunching economist running amuck in academic administration is sufficient to inspire concern, if not
fear, in many academic hearts. One is reminded of the
snicker of Kenneth Boulding (1970, 134), "No one in his
senses would want his daughter to marry an economic man."
    Economists do quantify many relationships, and such
quantifications often are both rigorous and useful. Quantified analyses often have great utility, for example, in
allocating scarce classroom space, in reaching conclusions
about whether female faculty suffer from salary discrimin-
ation, or in estimating the probable demand for a given
educational program. But economics is not mathematics.
Rather, economics is a logic that often utilizes mathematics, statistics, and the computer to produce evidence
and to test hypotheses generated by economic theory and
logic. The administrator who knows little mathematics but
understands economic logic will be immensely productive.
The reverse seems unlikely. Quantitative skills that are
not bounded and guided by economic logic produce little of
value because the correct questions are not being asked.
    The most important and influential course in the
training of any economist is the basic principles-of-economics sequence taught to collegiate freshmen and sopho-
mores. The principles-of-economics course presents, or at
least intimates, the essence of economic logic. Subse-
quent courses refine and extend that contribution but arguably never approach the high additional value of the
initial principles course (Siegfried and Fels 1979). The
point is that an administrator need not master advanced
economics, differential equations, or econometrics to pursue the logic outlined in this chapter, or to function as
a very respectable economist-administrator. The major
contribution of economics to the art and science of administration is the identification of a logical way of
dissecting and thinking about decision problems. Administrators who understand and can apply the basic principles
of economics have at their fingertips an immensely powerful logic to be utilized in a wide range of different academic situations.

FINAL WORDS

Let's now attempt to stand back a few paces from
these arguments. Disciplinary chauvinists who believe
that their own academic specialties contain the royal road
to civilization, tranquility, and happiness are, unfortu-
nately, a dime a dozen in a modern university. Economists, who have become somewhat imperialistic and univer-
sal in their analyses in recent years, are perhaps inclin-
ed to carry such intellectual coals to Newcastle (Becker
1976). Their tendency to view themselves as preachers in
possession of a secular gospel, and the current ascendancy
of many economists in both private sector and government
leadership posts, have been greeted with some cynicism by
many observers. "After all," one of my noneconomist colleagues has pointed out, "you could stretch all the economists in the world end to end and they would never reach a
conclusion. It's always 'on the one hand this, and on the
other hand that.'"

If the reader is willing to accept the view that economics is a way of approaching and thinking about a problem and not a published set of answers and conclusions,
these criticisms have less force. Instead, the focus
should be on whether economists, and economist-administrators, make better decisions. In this case, as in so
many others, the proof of the pudding is indeed primarily
reserved for the eating. And that, dear reader, is where
this chapter ends and your task of culinary judgment must
begin.

REFERENCES

Becker, Gary. 1976. The Economic Approach to Human
        Behavior. Chicago: University of Chicago Press.
Boulding, Kenneth. 1970. Economics as a Science. New
        York: McGraw-Hill.
Chizmar, John F., L. Dean Hiebert, and Bernard J. Mc-
        Carney. 1977. Assessing the impact of an instruc-
        tional innovation on achievement differentials: The
        case of computer-assisted instruction. Journal of
        Economic Education 9 (Fall):42–46.
Fall enrollment sets record despite fewer 18-year-olds.
        Chronicle of Higher Education 21 (Nov. 10):3.
Grabowski, Stanley M. 1981. Marketing in Higher Educa-
        tion. Washington, D.C.: ERIC-American Association
        for Higher Education.

Hoenack, Stephen A. 1982. Pricing and efficiency in
    higher education. Journal of Higher Education 58
    (July/Aug.):403-18.
Kotler, Philip. 1975. Marketing for Nonprofit Organiza-
    tions. Englewood Cliffs, N.J.: Prentice-Hall.
McKenzie, Richard B., and Gordon Tullock. 1978. Modern
    Political Economy: An Introduction to Economics.
    New York: McGraw-Hill.
Mayhew, Lewis B. 1979. Surviving the Eighties. San
    Francisco: Jossey-Bass.
Samuelson, Paul A. 1973. Economics. 9th ed. New York:
    McGraw-Hill.
Siegfried, John J., and Rendigs Fels. 1979. Research on
    teaching college economics: A survey. Journal of
    Economic Literature 17 (Sept.):923-69.
Skolnick, Michael L. 1980. Pricing as an element in uni-
    versity planning: Some principles and problems.
    Planning for Higher Education 9 (Nov.):18-24.
Stigler, George J. 1961. The economics of information.
    Journal of Political Economy 69 (June):213-25.

2   *Economic Trends in Health Care for the 1980s*

PAUL J. FELDSTEIN

For a number of years, hospitals have been considered a growth industry. Revenues have been increasing at better than 13 percent per year, the number of employees and their wages have been increasing relative to other sectors of the economy, and those industries supplying hospitals-- firms in the hospital supply and medical technology industries--have been the favorites of Wall Street investors. Even those hospitals that are organized for profit, the investor-owned chains, have been selling at higher- price-earning multiples than has the stock market as a whole. Is it likely that hospitals and the health care sector will continue to expand? Are hospitals insulated from the economic and demographic factors that affect the growth, maturity, and eventual decline of other industries?

To appreciate how hospitals are likely to change, it is necessary to determine the trends that affect both hospital revenues and costs. In addition, which trends increase more rapidly will influence whether hospitals continue to expand the services they offer or whether administrators, attending medical staffs, and the boards of trustees will have to make increasingly difficult choices as resources become scarcer.

It is probably easier to anticipate what is likely to happen to hospital costs than to hospital revenues. Cost

pressures are more likely to continue to increase than to
decrease. A lower inflation rate over the coming years
will lessen some of the cost pressures on hospitals. However, hospital costs have always exceeded the increase in
the consumer price index; it is likely they will continue
to do so. Health care is basically a service industry in
which productivity increases are difficult to achieve and
in which it is more difficult to substitute capital for
labor than in other industries. Continued progress in development of medical technology will also increase costs.
While in other industries improvements in technology result in greater productivity and hence decreased unit
costs, advances in medical technology result in the need
for more technically trained personnel and consequently
increased unit costs. In addition to this change in their
"product," hospitals are also experiencing a more expensive patient mix; the aged are an increasing percentage of
the patients.

    Will hospitals be able to pass these cost increases
on to the payors of hospital care as they have in the
past? Unless they are able to do so, the outlook is
bleak. To determine the answer, it is necessary to examine the forces that affect the trend in hospital revenues.

FORCES AFFECTING HOSPITAL REVENUES

    For an industry to be in the growth stage of its life
cycle, the factors affecting the demand for its services
must be increasing. Important to the demand for hospital
care is growth in both the population and in the percentage of the population with hospital insurance. Since population growth in this country is increasing by only 1
percent per year and a large portion of the population
currently has some form of third-party (either private or
public) coverage for hospital care, the overall growth in
the industry has slowed down. Changes in hospital revenue, therefore, will come from changes in reimbursement
and from changes in utilization rates. Hospital utilization has been increasing at a very slow rate, at less than
1 percent per year between 1975 and 1980. The utilization
of hospitals by those under 65 years of age has been declining while utilization by those over 65 has been increasing. The decline in hospital utilization by the nonaged is the result of factors that are likely to continue,
the changes in medical practice and the greater availability of nonhospital coverage. Another important trend is

the increase in the number of working women, which means a
delay in the age when women have children and to a smaller number of children.

Although hospital utilization by the aged is increasing, projected revenues from this age group are uncertain;
if anything, the rate of increase in reimbursement is
likely to decline. Hospital reimbursement for the aged
depends on government policy. When Medicare was introduced in the mid-1960s, government reimbursement was relatively generous; hospitals were reimbursed not only for
their costs of caring for the aged but were given an additional 2 percent. As a result, hospitals' financial positions improved. As government expenditures under Medicare
and Medicaid continued to increase, however, the federal
government (and state governments with large Medicaid populations) developed a greater interest in holding down the
rate of increase in hospital costs. It is estimated that
by 1982 the federal government was spending $90 billion on
these two programs, and these expenditures were increasing
at the rate of 18 percent per year.

There are several ways in which the rate of increase
in Medicare expenditures can be held down. The first is
to change eligibility requirements or benefits. Since
Medicare covers the aged, it would be politically difficult for Congress or any administration to reduce benefits, other than permitting slight increases in deduct-
ibles and copayments. A more politically acceptable approach is to increase benefits to include less costly out-
of-hospital substitutes, for example, including home care
as a reimbursable benefit and providing Medicare vouchers
for prepaid health care. Either of these proposals, if
enacted, would decrease hospital utilization. However,
the most immediate way in which government can reduce its
expenditures under Medicare is not paying the full amount
it owes hospitals for care of the aged. This last approach is being used today. Hospitals are increasingly
complaining that they are receiving less than their full
costs for Medicare patients. Third-party payors, particularly commercial insurance carriers, are concerned about
<u>cost</u> <u>shifting</u> (hospitals charging other payors of care
more because the government is paying less than its
share).

Since utilization by the aged is increasing and represents a greater portion of hospital utilization and reimbursement for the aged is less than full cost, hospitals' financial positions will deteriorate. And on the

horizon are possible changes in benefits that will reduce
hospital utilization by the aged. Further, the higher
hospital utilization rate by the aged, a mixed blessing
because of the government's reimbursement policies, may
decline in the years ahead if lower cost substitutes become available.

Hospitals also face a changing outlook with respect
to projected revenues from the nonaged. With the growth
in hospital insurance having already occurred and with the
relatively stable population base, hospitals appear to
have entered the "mature" stage of their industry life
cycle. They cannot count on continued increases in demand
by the nonaged as a source of additional revenues. There
are of course regional variations in growth in hospital
demand. The South and Southwest are growing in population, while the Northeast and Midwest are losing. Hospitals in these regions face quite different growth prospects.

Insurance companies and Blue Cross Associations are
also feeling the effects of limited growth in demand for
hospital insurance. Increased enrollment in one insurance
company can only come at the expense of another company's
market share. The health insurance market has become increasingly competitive. To compete with one another on a
premium basis, the insurance carriers and the Blues are
placing greater pressures on hospitals to hold down expenditures. Tighter hospital reimbursement and coverage for
lower cost substitutes for hospital care are examples of
these approaches.

Another source of concern for hospitals is the attempt by business and labor to hold down their health care
costs. Rising health costs increase a firm's health insurance premiums and consequently result in higher labor
costs to the firm. These higher costs, in turn, cause the
prices of goods and services sold by the industry to increase. As a result, there are decreases in the demand
for those goods and services as well as for the labor used
to produce them. To offset the growing cost of fringe
benefit programs, businesses and labor unions are becoming
more actively involved in holding down their community's
expenditures for health care. Business coalitions are being formed to coordinate the efforts of the payors of care
and place greater pressure on the providers to hold down
their costs and charges. Business and labor are also ex-
perimenting with self-insurance programs, lower cost substitutes for hospitalization, utilization review programs,

and alternatives to the fee-for-service system (namely, prepaid health care). The effect of all of these efforts will be a decrease in hospital utilization.

The trends of hospital utilization and hospital reimbursement are likely to be quite different in the 1980s than they were in the 1960s and 1970s.

THE CHANGING MARKET IN WHICH HOSPITALS COMPETE

A firm with a monopoly position in its area, even when it faces tighter reimbursement, does not have to worry about losing its market share to competitors. A firm in a very competitive industry, in addition to worrying about tighter reimbursement and declining utilization, also has to be concerned that competitors and substitute services may take away its market share. An important current phenomenon in health care is that more substitutes for hospital care are becoming available, along with sources of payment for their services.

Three trends are making the hospital industry more competitive.

The Increase in the Supply of Physicians

As a result of mandated enrollment increases (to qualify for federal funds), medical schools increased their enrollments through the 1970s. New medical schools were started, as well. The consequence of these capitation grants has been an increasing supply of physicians. The number of physicians increased 50 percent between 1965 and 1980 and is expected to increase another 40 percent over the coming decade. Such a large increase in both the absolute number of physicians and in the physician-population ratio should have an important impact on the delivery of medical services.

The increase in numbers means physicians will have an increasingly difficult time maintaining their real incomes. To some extent, physicians will be able to "create" increased demand for their services, but it is unlikely that physicians will be able to create sufficient demand to maintain their incomes. Evidence to support this belief is that the number of physician visits per capita over the last few years has not been increasing; on a per physician basis, physician visits are decreasing. Similarly, physician incomes over this period, adjusted for inflation, have been falling. Given the trends in declining government reimbursement for physician service and

the growth of health maintenance organizations (HMOs),
which "lock in" their patient populations, physicians will
have to develop new approaches if they are to maintain
their real incomes.

Physicians are likely to respond to this more competitive environment in the following ways. First, they will
attempt to increase the number of services they provide to
patients. This is likely to include an increase in the
number of tests prescribed for patients and an increase
in the range of services they offer, such as patient coun-
seling and education. Second, there will be greater competition among physicians for patients. This competition
is likely to take the form of physicians making their services more convenient and accessible to patients, for example, by lengthening office hours and locating in resi-
dential areas closer to patients. Physicians will also
try to develop a competitive advantage over other physicians. An example of this type of strategy is the attempt
by a medical staff to deny hospital staff privileges to
new physicians on the grounds they are not needed. Such
anticompetitive behavior will place the medical staff in
conflict with the hospital, which will need a larger supply of physicians in order to keep its beds filled. Third,
physicians are likely to try to restrict the professional
practices of other health professionals through changes in
the state practice acts. More political struggles are
likely to occur over which professions are legally permitted to perform certain tasks. Physicians' attempts to
limit encroachment on their market demand will likely lead
to conflicts between orthopedic surgeons and podiatrists,
ophthalmologists and optometrists, and physicians and
nurse practitioners.

As a fourth strategy, physicians are likely to engage
in competition with hospitals for patients. Physicians
will provide emergency services and set up ambulatory care
clinics to attract patients away from hospital outpatient
departments. They will also perform more outpatient surgery in their offices, which will decrease hospital utilization. The cost per hospitalized patient will consequently increase as the less costly patients are treated
on an ambulatory basis.

Fifth, physicians will be forced to consider how to
compete with HMOs and other alternative delivery systems.
Because of the greater physician supply, prepaid health
plans will find it easier to attract physicians. If, as
expected, there is an increase in the number of prepaid

plans and in their coverage of the population, physicians
may form their own prepaid plans in order to compete on a
premium basis. Physicians may also believe that they can
keep a greater portion of the premium for themselves if
they are able to reduce hospital utilization. These types
of competitive responses by physicians have been observed
in California and Minnesota, where there has been growth
in prepaid health plans. The effect on hospitals of the
growth in prepaid health plans has been a reduction in
their portion of the premium dollar from 54 percent, the
national average, to 34 percent.

Prepaid Health Plans
        Prepaid health plans are currently a small portion of
the health care market. Indications are, however, that
their growth will increase more rapidly. Both industry
and labor now have stronger incentives to experiment with
methods to reduce health care costs. Any federal initia-
tives in this area, such as a proposed voucher system for
the aged, will also serve to stimulate this trend. In the
Certificate of Need (CON) process, for example, an incentive has been provided to hospitals by granting them ex-
emptions if they have a high proportion of HMO patients.
Another factor that will make it easier for HMOs and prepaid health plans to grow is the increase in the number of
physicians. In the past, when the physician-to-population
ratio was much lower, physicians could earn a high rate of
return by practicing in the preferred fee-for-service system. Today many young physicians are willing to join prepaid health plans rather than incur the expense and uncer-
tainty of starting independent practices.
        The growth of prepaid health plans presents hospitals
with a major potential threat to their revenues. According to HMO proponents and to empirical studies, as well,
hospital utilization among HMO subscribers is approximately half that in the non-HMO population. As more of the
population moves into an HMO setting, therefore, there
will be a decreased demand for inpatient hospital services. The impact on hospitals will be not only a decrease in utilization and revenues but also a higher cost
per admission. As the less costly patients are treated on
an ambulatory basis, the average cost of care of those patients remaining in the hospital will increase.
        In areas where prepaid health plans have presented a
greater competitive threat to the fee-for-service system,
the existing health care providers have reacted by start-

ing their own prepayment plans. As more of the fee-for-
service system is brought under a prepaid arrangement,
these new prepaid plans will also attempt to lower the
hospital utilization of their subscribers. Thus the
growth of prepaid plans and the competitive reaction to
them by the fee-for-service system should serve to further
decrease hospital utilization and revenue.

Multi-institutional Systems

There have always been some hospitals affiliated with
others. The most obvious example is hospitals associated
with organized religious groups; in recent years for-prof-
it hospital chains have developed. An important current
development is the joining together of nonprofit hospitals
into what is referred to as multi-institutional systems.
What is surprising about such a development is that the
medical staff and the nonprofit hospital are willing to
surrender some autonomy and control in return for the benefits of affiliation. There are various degrees of hospital affiliation. The weakest form is one where hospitals
share certain hotel-type services (such as laundry facilities) or participate in a joint purchasing program. At
the other extreme is the hospital merger. The stronger
the degree of affiliation, the greater the loss of autonomy by both the hospital and its medical staff. Presum-
ably, the benefits from affiliation are at least equal to
the loss in autonomy by the affiliating hospital. Hospitals and their medical staff prefer to be autonomous; thus
they would be willing to trade autonomy only for at least
an equivalent amount of benefits.

The structure of the hospital industry is changing,
becoming more concentrated. As more hospitals enter into
affiliation agreements, the share of the hospital market
served by such multi-institutional systems has increased.
To understand the type of industry in which hospitals will
be competing and whether the degree of concentration is
likely to become even greater, it is important to analyze
the reasons for these changes in the hospital industry.
There are two basic reasons why an industry changes its
structure: greater economies of scale, and the need for
increased revenues.

In past years, when demand for hospital care was increasing and hospitals were reimbursed generously on a
cost-plus basis, hospitals were able to increase their
revenues and were under little pressure to contain costs.
Currently, the environment in which hospitals compete has

changed. For hospitals to grow, and for some even to survive, they need to take advantage of any possible cost
savings as well as new sources of revenues.

Potential cost savings from affiliation with other
hospitals are found in several areas. There are economies
of scale in joint activities such as purchasing agreements, data processing systems, and building and equipping
of hospitals. To benefit from such cost savings, the hospital must enter into some form of agreement with other
institutions. However, since it is not necessary for the
hospital to give up much autonomy in order to benefit from
such sharing arrangements, these types of activities are
characterized by the most limited, or weakest, types of
affiliation. To take advantage of further cost savings
requires the hospital to belong to a more tightly affiliated system, with a consequently greater loss of autonomy.
These cost savings are generally financial. In larger
hospital systems, for example, lower interest charges on
bond issues are possible, as is improved cash management
through interhospital borrowing. In addition, averaging
risks over larger patient populations can reduce malprac-
tice premiums.

The need for additional revenue is also an important
reason for restructuring the hospital industry. Sometimes
a hospital faces a stable demand for its services, as, for
example, a teaching hospital located in a declining urban
area. To increase its revenues and to ensure the use of
its services, such a hospital may acquire, or affiliate
with, smaller hospitals in surrounding areas. The need
for horizontal integration (that is, hospitals seeking to
acquire or affiliate with other hospitals) depends on the
part of the country in which the hospital is located. In
the South and Southwest, the growth in hospital revenues
is generally sufficient to enable hospitals to remain independent. In the Midwest, many hospitals are realizing
that unless they are willing to give up part of their autonomy and become part of a larger system, they will not
be able to survive.

Hospitals prefer to seek new sources of revenue rather than to relinquish autonomy. There is thus a movement
by hospitals to diversify into new lines of business;
their organizations have been restructured so that revenues from new services are kept separate from inpatient
services. As a result of such restructuring, new sources
of revenue are not included in calculations for Medicare
reimbursement nor are they subject to state hospital regulation.

The growth in multi-institutional systems has been
rapid. The hospital affiliation agreements being developed, however, are not uniform. Some hospitals are very
tightly controlled by the system to which they belong,
while others are not. It is difficult to predict trends
in these types of agreements. Only for a compelling reason are hospitals and medical staffs willing to give up
their autonomy. Thus we are more likely to observe loose
affiliations allowing the hospital to take advantage of
cost savings from economies of scale. Hospitals in financial difficulty, either because of falling demand or
tighter reimbursement limits, will be more willing to
trade autonomy for survival. Thus the growth of these
multisystems depends on the particular situation in which
hospitals find themselves. Indications are that as economies of scale increase, the industry will become more
concentrated. Unaffiliated hospitals may be at a competitive disadvantage if they have higher costs.

As the concentration of the hospital industry increases, multihospital systems will have to be more aware
of the possible antitrust implications of their competitive behavior. Mergers that increase a systems' market
share in an area may be characterized by competitors as
attempts to monopolize the market. Hospitals will have to
become familiar with economic definitions of markets and
what constitutes substitute services if they are to defend
themselves successfully against antitrust suits.

SUMMARY OF TRENDS IN THE ECONOMIC OUTLOOK FOR HOSPITALS

While the use of the hospital by the aged has been
increasing, government reimbursement has become much
tighter. As Medicare and Medicaid come to represent a
larger portion of hospital utilization, hospitals are attempting to increase their revenues by seeking higher pay-
ments from nongovernment third-party payors. Insurance
companies, the Blues, business, and labor, however, are
attempting to lower the rate of increase in their premiums
by decreasing hospital costs of their subscribers, employees, or union members. Tighter controls on reimbursement,
utilization control systems, lower cost substitutes to
hospitalization, and alternative delivery systems are
examples of such approaches. The effect of both government and private sector efforts to reduce health care expenditures has been to limit the growth in hospital revenues.

Hospital cost increases, while related to the rate of

inflation in the economy, are likely to be difficult to
limit even if the inflation rate slows down. Increases in
medical technology will continue to increase the cost of
medical equipment; declining younger age cohorts in the
population will result in a smaller supply of nurses and,
consequently, in higher wages for nurses. Government subsidies for capital and health manpower, which in the past
have held down hospital cost increases, are being phased
out. Hospitals will find it increasingly difficult to increase revenues to offset increases in costs.

     With respect to the markets in which hospitals com-
pete, they are facing increased competition from the larger supply of physicians, who are seeking to increase their
own revenues by performing more hospital services in their
own offices. The growth in HMOs will decrease hospital
utilization. Multihospital systems, with their cost advantages and their search for additional revenues, will
increase the competitive pressures on the free-standing
community hospital. Concentration in the hospital sector
is likely to increase. Not all regions of the country nor
all hospitals are experiencing the same revenue and competitive pressures. Revenue growth is more difficult in
the Northeast and Midwest. As the less severely ill are
treated in lower cost hospitals, teaching hospitals will
find they are left with the more expensive cases; their
cost per patient will rise even faster, leaving them with
the problem of finding additional revenue to continue patient care, teaching, and research functions. Public hospitals, so dependent on government for operating funds,
will also find it increasingly difficult to survive in the
coming decade. In a growing number of regions of the
United States, hospitals have become a mature industry.
Their growth in utilization is leveling off and may actually decline. New revenue sources are likely to become an
increasing concern in the years ahead.

ECONOMIC CHOICES FACING HOSPITALS
     Hospitals and other health care providers face three
options in the coming years. Limited increases in hospital revenues, rising costs, and increasing competition
will force many institutions to seek a merger with a
stronger organization. Becoming part of a larger health
care system will be the only option available for many
providers. Hospitals and medical staffs choosing this option will have less autonomy.

     Other hospitals with the same economic outlook may

use a different strategy for survival, seeking protection
through legislation. Entry controls on new hospitals (to
prevent them from entering their markets) and on rate
regulation (to ensure payment for services) can be proposed to ensure the hospitals' existence. An even stronger
legislative mandate would make hospitals equivalent to
public utilities. In this case, hospitals would be fran-
chised to serve a given population; such a franchise would
preclude competitors from entering their markets and would
guarantee the institution a budget to serve that population.

Protection through legislation is an attractive alternative to many hospitals, such as attempting to influence the state's allocation of funds to hospitals. Based
on the evidence of CON programs, hospitals have not been
adversely affected by such legislation; in fact, they were
able to turn it to their advantage by precluding entry of
proprietary institutions. Hospitals were also not adversely affected by many of the state rate review programs. The early hospital reimbursement negotiations
under Medicare also proved very advantageous to hospitals.
However, currently under Medicare and in stringent rate-
review states such as New York, some hospitals' financial
conditions are deteriorating.

Initially hospitals have received favorable treatment
under regulatory frameworks. However, as additional
groups such as state governments, business, labor, and
insurance companies develop a concentrated interest in
holding down health care costs, compromise decisions are
reached by legislatures and hospitals do not do as well.
Their reimbursement becomes tighter, and their financial
position begins to decline. As other interests begin to
dominate the regulatory process, hospitals find that regulation is used to freeze their budgets. Rate review, as
used in New York State, will become typical for regulated
hospitals. As regulation limits hospital revenue, the
growth in health care expenditures will occur outside the
regulated sector. Other organizations, not subject to
regulatory constraints, will be able to innovate and offer
profitable services. Regulated hospitals will find themselves in a shrinking market.

Escaping economic competition through legislative
protection may guarantee an institution's survival. However, regulation provides an institution neither sufficient funds nor the flexibility to allow it to innovate in
health care delivery. Instead, hospitals and other health

care providers may realize that the rewards are fairer and
the system more efficient when the outcomes are determined
by economic rather than political competition.

Thus the third type of strategy that hospitals may
adopt to survive and even to grow is engaging in economic
competition. To prosper under competition, hospitals must
be able to secure new sources of revenue. To do so they
must diversify into new services. There are three types
of services hospitals should consider. The first is increasing the number of feeder systems into the hospital.
To keep occupancy high, hospitals will require a larger
patient base. A hospital can actively seek referrals for
hospital utilization from primary care physicians. To
accomplish this, a hospital should increase the number of
primary care physicians on its staff and develop free-
standing emergency centers and ambulatory care clinics in
outlying areas. Such a strategy, however, can result in a
conflict; if the hospital attempts to add physicians to
its staff, the existing medical staff may attempt to retain their competitive advantage over other physicians by
denying them hospital privileges. It is important for the
hospital to realize that on this issue its economic interests may diverge from those of the exisiting medical
staff. A hospital unable to increase its pool of primary
care physicians will find it difficult to maintain its
occupancy rate in a period when hospital utilization rates
are declining. With the increase in physician supply, the
relatively low ratio of physicians to hospitals is changing, so hospitals should be able to set the conditions for
staff privileges.

The second type of services hospitals can diversify
into are those considered to be substitutes for hospital
care. Outpatient surgery decreases the demand for hospital inpatient care. To the extent that there is an increase in the use of outpatient surgery, hospitals will be
left with the more costly inpatient surgical cases increasing the average cost for surgery in the hospital. To
prevent the loss of revenues from outpatient surgery, hospitals should provide this service; as their use increases, hospitals will have little choice but to offer
them. Another substitute for hospital care is the HMO. As
HMOs attract more subscribers in an area, hospitals will
experience decreases in utilization. (Again, the remaining cost per inpatient admission will increase as the less
costly admissions are cared for on an outpatient basis.)
To prevent this loss of revenue, hospitals can either

start or affiliate with an HMO. Not only would the HMO
use the hospital for its inpatient services but the hospital might also share in noninpatient revenue, which will
become an increasing portion of the premium. As government and insurance companies seek to lower their premiums
for health care, it is likely that more lower cost substitutes for hospitalization will be covered as insurance
benefits. If hospitals are to maintain their revenues,
it is essential that they become providers of these substitute services.

The third type of diversification hospitals should
consider is offering nonacute care services. Hospitals
are primarily involved in the provision of acute care, but
there is a growing demand for nonacute health-related services, for example, wellness clinics and screening programs, such as hypertension and diabetes control and vision and hearing testing. Hospitals may find, as well, a
growing market in industry for occupational health services. Another important set of services for which there
is a growing demand is services to the aged. The aged
population is one of the most rapidly growing population
groups in society. There are currently 24 million persons
over 65 years of age. At the end of the decade it is estimated there will be 30 million aged. Among the aged,
the fastest growing group are those greater than 75 years
of age. It is expected that this group will increase by
30 percent, from 9 million currently to 12 million by
1990. As federal and state governments seek to lower
their costs for caring for the aged, lower cost substitutes to inpatient care will become reimbursable. A growing number of aged will be able to finance such services
themselves. The aged will continue to be an important
health care market, although not just in terms of inpatient utilization. Hospitals could provide health-related
services to the noninstitutionalized aged through home
health care and retirement centers, for example.

The provision of such nonacute services requires the
hospital to develop a different perspective of the industry it is part of. Acute inpatient care should be viewed
as only one service in a spectrum of health care services.
Hospitals should become vertically integrated organizations, responsible for all of a person's health needs--
from the well person to services for the aged. Unless the
hospital changes the view of its mission to that of a
health care corporation, it will not be able to perceive
the markets, population groups, and services for which it

should be competing. A long-term strategy must be based
on a clear vision of the organization's mission.

CONCLUSION
     All industries have a life cycle--stages of growth,
maturity, and decline--and so do the firms that are part
of that industry. Unless the firms have an appreciation
of the changes occurring in the environment in which they
compete, they are likely to shrink in size, merge with
other declining firms, or simply go out of business. At
times such changes occur slowly. At other times, as when
there is a change in legislation affecting an industry,
the changes occur very rapidly. The brokerage and airlines industries are examples of industries that have un-
dergone rapid change as a result of deregulation. Some
new firms have prospered, while some established firms
have merged or gone out of business. Whenever an industry
faces such changes in its life cycle or in its environment, some firms manage to survive and even prosper. In
the health care industry, those hospitals with a clear vision of their mission and the changing environment in
which they compete are likely to survive and grow.

3 *The Economics of the Corporation*

ALVIN J. KARCHERE

The theory of the firm, as discussed by economists, has two aspects. It provides a useful box of tools for decision making. As a consequence, business administration majors who have been able to master the relationship between marginal and average costs and understand the meaning of the elasticity of demand have a competitive advantage over their colleagues who do not. The theory also can be thought of as a description of reality, or at least a reasonably close approximation. It is the relationship between what economists have to say about the firm and reality that is my subject.

TEXTBOOK THEORY OF THE FIRM

In the textbooks, industries are classified as being perfectly competitive, oligopolistic, or monopolistic (Samuelson 1980). In the perfectly competitive industries there are many producers and buyers of nearly identical products, and prices are determined in markets by the many buyers and sellers. The firms in the industry attempt to achieve an equilibrium position that maximizes profits. In equilibrium, at the price determined by the market, the firms' marginal costs and long-run average costs equal the price. That point represents the optimal use of resources by society. In terms of their social consequences, according to the textbooks, the other forms of industrial organization are inferior to perfect competition. Unregulated monopoly in equilibrium enjoys excess profits by setting a price that is too high and output that is too low to achieve a social optimum. Oligopoly is competition

among the few. Unlike perfect competition, there is no
unique equilibrium solution in oligopoly. The outcome depends on the number of oligopolistic competitors in the
industry and what each assumes about the others' response
to given pricing or other competitive action. It also depends on the ease of entry of new competitors. Under the
most unfavorable conditions the equilibrium outcome approaches monopoly and under the most favorable it approaches perfect competition. Industries may also be organized in another form that the textbooks call monopolistic competition. In this form there may be many sellers
and easy entry but each sells a product that differs in
some respect from the others'. The long-run equilibrium
solution in this case is characterized by absence of competitive profits and by excess costs caused by wasteful
use of capacity (Samuelson 1980).

The textbooks generally agree that only a relatively
small fraction of the United States economy is characterized by perfect competition and that most of it should be
described in terms of oligopoly and monopolistic competition. Thus it follows that if consumer wants are satisfied with maximum efficiency only in perfect competitive
conditions, then in most of the U.S. economy wants are
satisfied with less than optimal efficiency and that,
therefore, economic policy should move the economy toward
perfect competiton.

THREE CRITICISMS OF THE TEXTBOOK THEORY
    This theory of the individual corporation and the in-
dustry is generally viewed as less than satisfactory, and
there have been various criticisms of it. Herbert Simon
(1959) leveled telling arguments against the textbook
theory of the firm. He rejected the key assumption in
this theory, which is that corporations strive to maximize
profits. His alternative theory assumed that "the firm's
goal is not maximizing profit but attaining a certain level or rate of profit, holding a certain share of the market or a certain level of sales. Firms would try to satisfice rather than maximize." Moreover, he does not believe that an analysis based on comparing equilibrium positions is very useful because most corporations live in a
dynamic environment where consumer tastes, competition,
and technology are changing rapidly. In these circumstances there is no a priori reason to believe in the attainment of equilibrium. An alternative to decision-

making theories based on striving for and attaining maximum profits in long-run equilibrium are theories derived from psychology. They suggest that when performance falls short of the level of aspiration a search for new alternative actions and, perhaps, an adjustment of the goal take place. If these changes are not satisfactory, neurosis replaces rational adaptive behavior.

Simon makes another fundamental criticism of the textbook theory of the firm. That theory deals with choice between fixed and known alternatives. Simon believes that the theory of the economic decision process must deal with alternatives that are not given but are sought and that the theory must take into account the difficulties and uncertainties of determining the consequences of each alternative. In summary, Simon believes that "economic man is a satisficing animal whose problem solving is based on search activity to meet certain aspiration levels rather than a maximizing animal whose problem solving involves finding the best alternatives in terms of specified criteria." In terms of the theory of the firm, the satisficing model does not lead to the conclusion of efficiency in resource allocation that is derived from the theory of perfect competition.

Another critic of the textbook treatment of the theory of the firm is John Kenneth Galbraith, in his book, "The New Industrial State" (1967). According to Galbraith the economy is, broadly speaking, divided into two parts: the industrial system, characterized by large corporations and oligopoly, and the area outside the industrial system, which includes activities such as the small retail stores, repairmen, barbers, and dairy farmers. The latter operate within the market system. Farmers, for example, need not anticipate their demands for seed, fertilizer and pesticides, or spare parts for their machinery. The market stocks and supplies them. They do not set their prices; the market takes all their output at the ruling price. The characteristics of the industrial economy are much different. Here markets are extensively replaced by planning. Demand projections are made and consumers are controlled by advertising so that the projections are realized. The product prices are planned and controlled by the corporation. Provision is made for the supply of things needed for production: technology, plant and equipment, labor, raw materials, and semifinished products. The cost of these resources is planned and controlled by the corporation. In Galbraith's view, the

characteristics of the industrial sector of the economy
that require planning are advanced technology and the long
time span needed for the development and production of industrial products.

Moreover, according to Galbraith, the complexity of
the modern industrial corporation makes it impossible for
one person to control it. Decisions are made by commit-
tees and merely ratified by the top management. The com-
mittees are made up of specialists, such as development
engineers and scientists, industrial engineers, and financial and marketing experts. This group Galbraith named
collectively the "technostructure."

The main concern of the decision makers in the technostructure is not profit maximization but protection of a
minimum level of return. If they cannot accomplish this,
they lose their autonomy and their positions are threatened. The new industrial state, as Galbraith saw it, does
not achieve optimum efficiency in the allocation of resources. It does not even try to do that; but nevertheless, in Galbraith's mind, "There is little doubt as to
the ability of the industrial system to serve man's material needs . . . abundantly."

John Galbraith and Herbert Simon both rejected the
notion that the corporation is the rational maximizer of
textbook theory. This view was supported by Gunnar
Eliasson's survey of corporate planning. Eliasson studied
sixty-two large corporations, thirty of them U.S. and
thirty-two non-U.S. firms (Eliasson 1976).

A planning and accounting system designed to maximize
profits must supply the data needed for analysis and make
the calculations required to determine when maximums are
attained. Eliasson did not find this kind of evidence.
What he did find were planning systems that set targets
based on past performance; his conclusion was that corporations plan to "maintain or improve performance" rather
than maximize profits. This finding was consistent with
Herbert Simon's hypothesis that firms satisfice.

When Eliasson began his study on company planning it
was his assumption that the planning system would be a
method for marshalling the best research in the company on
such matters as demand elasticities and supply and cost
functions, and that planning decisions would be made ob-
jectively, based on the evidence provided by the studies.
His conclusion was that the plans were the results of
"bargaining between conflicting parties in the organiza-
tional hierarchy rather than through 'objective'

research." He found that the main purpose of planning was
to make it possible for the corporate leadership to dele-
gate routine decisions from the corporate headquarters to
the operating units. Planning was a procedure for agree-
ing on objectives and then delegating responsibility for
the achievement of those objectives to the operating unit
managements. The purpose of this was to allow scope for
individual initiative in executing a plan while retaining
ultimate corporate management control.

Eliasson also discovered that corporation managements
felt that the planning system was "more or less useless
for handling large, unstructured innovative decisions."
Indeed a major purpose of the planning system was to dele-
gate authority and thus free up corporate management time
so that it could be applied to unique, ill-structured
problems and opportunities.

THE THEORY OF CONTESTABLE MARKETS
     The common thread in the criticisms by Simon, Gal-
braith, and Eliasson of standard textbook theory is the
rejection of profit maximization as a realistic description of business behavior. This conclusion, of course,
implies that the tight, elegant theoretical analysis of
the standard theory of the firm is largely irrelevant as a
description of economic behavior. William Baumol and his
associates, taking another track, have recently developed
a new theory that preserves the methodology of standard
economics (Baumol 1982). It is based on the assumption of
optimization and uses the standard analytical tools,
Baumol's criticisms of the standard theory point out that
in the standard theory, economic welfare is maximized under conditions of perfect competition but that the conditions required for perfect competition do not exist in
most industries and under conditions of oligopoly the results in terms of economic welfare depend on the assumptions made about the reactions and expectations of the
corporations in the industry. The standard theory fails
as a generalization because it relates to the corporations
already in the industry. In Baumol's new theory the analytical results are obtained by focusing on potential competitors.

     The new approach is called the theory of contestable
markets, those "into which entry is absolutely free and
exit is absolutely costless." There are no abnormal profits in a contestable market because if abnormal profits

are earned by incumbents in the industry potential competitors will enter the industry, make a profit, and, if
necesary, leave it.   Secondly, in contestable markets the
incumbents must be efficient.   Lack of efficiency will
create profit opportunities for new entrants.   Thirdly, in
contestable markets price equals marginal cost and, therefore, predatory prices cannot be used as in unfair competition.   If price is less than marginal cost in a contestable market and the incumbents are profitable, a new entrant can produce less than the incumbents, have lower
marginal costs and lower prices, be profitable, and increase market share at the expense of the incumbent.   If
price is greater than marginal cost a new entrant can increase market share by pricing at marginal cost.   Thus, in
a perfectly contestable market, price equals marginal cost
in equilibrium and production is efficient.

One of the claims that Baumol made for his new theory
is that it is a generalization of the theory of perfect
competition because perfect contestability theory is applicable without modification to oligopolistic markets.
To achieve these results Baumol must make two strong assumptions.   The first has to do with the cost of exit;
perfect contestability has to assume that a new entrant
who desires to leave the industry will be able to sell any
assets at their book value.   This implies it is possible
to leave without cost.   Thus a prospective new entrant who
sees the possibility of profit can seize it, even if it is
a temporary one.   It is the fear of such hit-and-run tac-
tics that keeps the incumbents efficient and provides a
motive for them to keep their prices at levels that avoid
abnormal profits.   The second assumption is that the incumbents will not respond to a new entrant by lowering
their prices.   Baumol does not suggest that these assumptions are realistic but that these assumptions are made to
examine the "properties of a market in which entry and
exit can occur costlessly and more rapidly than somewhat
sticky prices can change in response. . . . contestability
is merely a broader ideal, a benchmark of wider applicability than is perfect competition."

The assumptions that Baumol makes are necessary to
reach his conclusions about the properties of perfect contestable markets.   In a sense they are the price he has to
pay for rigorous, logically correct conclusions.   On the
question of how accurately pure contestability describes
the U.S. economy, Baumol states that the industry structures that actually do exist "will constitute reasonable

approximations to the efficient structures." He points
out however that he has little evidence on which to base
that conclusion.

REASONS FOR THE PERSISTENCE OF THE TEXTBOOK THEORY
     Given the criticisms that have been made of the stan-
dard theory, I am puzzled by its persistence.
     Part of the answer, I believe, can be found in the
economists' interest in the major problem addressed by the
standard theory. What could be more interesting than an
understanding of how the system as a whole works? Moreover, the discovery that perfect competition optimizes
economic welfare is a comforting conclusion. Finally, the
power and elegance of the mathematics that allow economists to discover the properties of perfect competition
provide a sense of professional satisfaction. The difficulty with all this is that economists also understand
that the conditions required for perfect competition apply
in only a small fraction of the U.S. economy. There is,
as well, no easy bridge from perfect competition to imperfect competition and oligopoly, and the satisfying conclusions that can be derived from the assumptions underlying
perfect competition cannot be extended to imperfect competition and oligopoly. Finally, there is no reasonable
set of policies that will transform an economy predominantly characterized by monopolistic competition and oligopoly into an economy that satisfies the conditions required for perfect competition.
     Another reason may help account for the persistence
of standard theory; it lies in the distinction between
positive and normative science. Although the standard
theory may be considered a failure as positive science because its conclusions about the economic welfare properties of an economy organized in perfectly competitive industries bear little resemblance to reality, that does not
prevent it from being useful as normative theory. An important set of problems are amenable to the tools economists have developed in the study of the theory of the
firms. Knowledge of the distinctions between average and
marginal cost and their relationship to average and marginal revenue and the properties of the cost and demand
functions that are required to reach optimum solutions is
useful for dealing with difficult behavioral problems.
Economists trained in microeconomics and the theory of the
firm can handle problems that cross a wide variety of

business functions and bring insights to bear on these
problems that sometimes are not accessible to the specialists in such functions as marketing, engineering, and
finance.

ARE CORPORATIONS OPTIMIZERS?

Even though economists find the theory of the firm
useful in the analysis of normative business problems,
Gunnar Eliasson has concluded from his study of large
corporations that firms do not keep their accounting rec-
ords or their planning data in forms that allow it to be
used for marginal analysis and optimization studies. That
conclusion is consistent with my own more limited observa-
tions. If marginal analysis and optimization are useful,
why are they not in more general use in business? Why do
they remain tools only of economists and management scientists?

To answer this question, it helps to examine those
areas where optimization techniques have been installed
and are in constant use. Optimization has been used successfully in the planning and operation of oil refineries,
chemical plants, steel mills, electrical power systems,
and transportation systems. The optimization techniques
used in these areas are generally not derived from the
calculus that forms the basis of most economic theory, but
from linear and nonlinear programming. That, however, is
a detail of little significance. Situations where optimization techniques have been applied have three characteristics: the processes to be optimized can be fully specified, they are repetitive, and they are complex enough to
be beyond judgmental methods. In the models employed to
make the optimization calculations, the nature of the production process is delineated and the model is solved for
minimum cost of production or for the mix of outputs that
earns maximum profits.

Now consider a different business problem, one that
is common in the present environment where innovation and
technical change rather than repetition are commonplace.
Given a period long enough to develop new products, how do
we discover the best product strategy? If the possible
list of products was complete it would be possible to conceive of this as an optimization problem. It would be a
different optimization problem from that described in
standard economic theory because it is likely that we
would have to deal with a number of production functions

rather than find the optimum scale of production for one
function. This is a possible but very difficult undertaking. However, we have not yet come to the heart of the
problem. The key to success in the discovery of the best
list of products is not the calculation of an optimum from
a given list. The critical point is that it is always
possible that a product not on the list, the product that
no one has yet been clever enough to think of, will be the
winner in the future. In this case, as in most others
where innovation is possible, the calculation of an optimum after the most important business decisions have been
made is of secondary importance. And this is one of the
important reasons why corporations do not expend the resources needed to make calculations of the optimum.

There is another, and perhaps equally important, reason why such calculations of the optimum are not made in
business planning. A large detailed mathematical model of
the corporation would be necessary, one that would have to
be updated each time a new plan was calculated with demand
and production functions for the new products in the product strategy and for innovations in the production process. It would be possible to build a model of this kind
and to update it for changes in the product strategy. The
work required is not for the fainthearted but could be
done in this age of large-scale computers. In a planning
system of this kind the central planning department of the
corporation would collect inputs, in great detail, from
the operating units and then, after solving the model for
the optimum plan, issue the appropriate instructions to
the operating unit staffs.

Anyone with the least experience in these matters has
by now come to the conclusion that this is an unworkable
procedure. There is little likelihood that such a model
would be accurate at the level of detail needed to make a
workable plan. Moreover, even if the technical problems
could be overcome, the people required to execute the plan
would have little faith in it and at the first indication
of difficulty they would blame "that stupid plan" developed by a computer imposed on them. Planners know that developing a plan is the smallest part of the problem. The
name of the game is execution. The probability of good
execution of a plan is increased if the people who have
the responsibility have been sufficiently involved in developing it to have confidence in it.

In IBM we carry this to the extreme: the plan is
generally made by the people who have the responsibility

for carrying it out. This is a time-consuming process, so
time-consuming that we find it difficult to consider many
alternatives. In a company committed to excellence, I
don't recall the corporate director of planning ever making the claim that the plan constructed under his management was the best of all possible plans. He would say it
was a good plan, or an excellent plan, not the optimum
plan.

EVALUATION OF CRITICISMS OF THE TEXTBOOK THEORY
     Much of what I have said about optimization is con-
sistent with Herbert Simon's work; I have included Herbert
Simon in my short list of critics of the standard or textbook theory of the firm because I agree with much of what
he says. I have included Kenneth Galbraith for the opposite reason, although as a participating member of the IBM
technostructure I would like to believe that the technostructure has the power and influence that Galbraith at-
tributes to it. Consider the relationship between the top
management of a corporation and the technostructure. According to Galbraith the top management is all but power-
less when confronted by the technostructure. The problems
are so complex and require such detailed expertise that
the management has no alternative but to ratify the rec-
ommendations of the technostructure. Perhaps there are
such spineless top managements, but relatively simple
techniques can make it unnecessary for managements to be
this weak.
     Galbraith seems to assume that business decisions are
so clear-cut that the technostructure can easily agree on
them. The contrary is usually the case. The future is
always uncertain. Well-informed people frequently have
different views about how to deal with those uncertainties. It is almost impossible to conceive of a top management so remote from the life of the corporation it manages that it is oblivious to the debate that is always going on in the company. Even if there were no formal method to hear alternative points of view, it would take only
a little questioning to gather such informtion.
     It is not difficult to formalize the flow of informa-
tion on the alternative possibilities in an uncertain future. The examples that follow, illustrate the fundamental situation; if these techniques weren't available,
someone would invent them. The first example is a technique for allowing alternative points of view to reach top

management. One of the simplest methods is to require the
preparation of option papers that outline the advantages
and disadvantages of various courses of action. In IBM we
have a system of contention that provides alternative
points of view on proposals that go to top management.
The advocate of a plan presents it to the top management
and frequently in the same meeting those who disagree with
the plan have an opportunity to outline their arguments.
In this situation the management is not a captive of the
technostructure but uses the technostructure to provide it
with the information it needs to make an informed decision.

Gunnar Eliasson's findings on the role of the planning system in corporate decision making is relevant here.
Eliasson concluded that corporate plans were little more
than summaries of the consequences of decisions that had
already been made by top management. He concluded that
the important business decisions, those dealing with
events that were highly uncertain or with major innovations, were handled by the top management outside the context of the formal planning system. If the technostructure is responsible for the development of formal plans,
as I think is the case, this tells us something of the
roles of the technostructure and the top management.

While Galbraith's view of the role of the technostructure is interesting, it is not the main point in his
argument. The main thrust concerns the relationship between the corporation and markets. As he sees it, markets
are replaced by corporate planning. In a certain sense
this is true. The large corporations do not buy their raw
materials and supplies or sell their products in markets
organized like the wheat market. In a word, the large
corporations do not operate in perfectly competitive markets. But that assertion is far removed from Galbraith's
claim that corporate planning supersedes markets, if we
mean by markets the interaction of buyers and sellers in
the economy. That interaction, of course, can and does
take place without formal organization. For example,
there is no market for automobiles organized like the
wheat market. Nevertheless, consumers react to the prices
of various makes of automobiles and manufacturers adjust
their prices and production schedules in response to the
behavior of consumers and their competitors. In this com-
monly accepted sense, there is a market for automobiles.

Galbraith appears to mean that corporations are able
to control these market forces and that they use their

planning systems to do so. It may well be true that corporations attempt to remain in control of their own des-
tiny; they attempt to enlarge their business and remain
profitable. It is obvious, however, that some do it better than others. Some corporations continue to grow and
are profitable in good economic times and bad, at least
for a period of time, while other corporations see their
business contracting and their profits shrinking and some
are driven to the wall and become bankrupt. In these circumstances it is clear that corporate planning does not
control the market. There remain market forces that reward companies offering products that consumers want at
prices attractive relative to those of their competitors.

From the perspective of the planner, it is impossible
to control a phenomenon if you cannot forecast the consequences of what the corporation does to try to control it.
Any corporation planner who has been plying the trade long
enough to have some experience knows the main characteristic of forecasts is that they are generally wrong to
some degree, sometimes badly wrong. Moreover, the major
discontinuities from past experience are hardly ever forecast correctly in corporate plans. These are the developments that have major impacts on the corporation fortunes.
They generally are not forecast correctly because, by
their nature, discontinuities rarely occur. Even if a
forecaster predicts one, the corporate plans will generally ignore the prediction because the probability of forecasting a major discontinuity correctly is very low.

In these circumstances, Galbraith's thesis that corporate planning supersedes the market is hardly credible.

It was the intention of Baumol and his associates "to
provide a unifying framework for a pure theory of industrial organization where none was available before."
Their work in contestable markets does that. To achieve
their results they have made assumptions that imply that
the main disciplinary force on incumbents in an industry
is the fear of hit-and-run raids by potential competitors.
This is made possible by free entry into the industry and
costless exit from it. Moreover, to attract potential
competition into the industry and also to make the theory
independent of the incumbents' reactions, the assumption
is made that the incumbents will not reduce their prices
to defend their market shares.

The realism of these assumptions is difficult to defend, and the concept of the hit-and-run raid as the main
enforcer of contestable markets is hard to accept. An

alternative hypothesis, one that retains the distinction
between incumbents and potential competitors, seems more
believable and is one that could be tested by appropriate
research. It is more plausible to assume that corporations move into new markets when they believe they have or
can develop a level of costs, an expected rate of improvement in costs, and a rate of product innovation that will
enable them to compete successfully with the incumbents
over the long run. In making that assessment, they take
into account the profits of the incumbent companies to determine what would happen to incumbents' cost of capital
if they were to cut prices to meet the new competition and
what the effects on the incumbents' competitive positions
would be if their cost of capital were to increase.

The incumbents, because of fear of potential competition, attempt to remain as efficient and innovative as
they possibly can and avoid profits that are excessively
attractive to competitors. Balanced against this is the
desire to achieve a low cost of capital. To discourage
potential competitors the incumbents would have to keep up
with or even stay ahead of the state of the art of manufacturing technology and marketing and other managerial
innovations. They would have to improve the quality and
other characteristics of their products as well as develop
new products.

What really matters in this competitive struggle is
innovation in production and management and the improvement and development of new products. What also matters
is how well the various functions of the corporation are
carried out. All things being equal, the corporation that
does an excellent job in all respects will be more successful than one that is sloppy in execution. Standard
economic theory handles these topics badly or not at all.
In particular, when the chief concern is innovation, as
argued earlier, optimization is not an appropriate concept
because the best innovation may be one that a search did
not discover.

One other conclusion of immense importance may be derived from Baumol's concept of incumbents and potential
competitors. It involves the role of international trade.

There are two main arguments for free international
trade: (1) the improvement in the standard of living resulting from the gains of free trade due to specialization
and (2) the improvement in productivity stimulated by foreign competition in a regime of free trade. The second
argument takes on new significance in light of the theory

of contestable markets. In a country as large as the
United States the number of potential competitors for any
given industry is greater than it would be in a smaller
country. This, perhaps, accounts for the vitality of the
U.S. economy when compared with some others. But corporations in even small countries, such as the Netherlands,
can be efficient and innovative when the country practices
free trade. In those circumstances the corporations of
the small country must be able to impress potential competitors with their vitality and efficiency to avoid being
overwhelmed by foreign competitors. Viewed from this
point of view the actual and potential competition with
American business from Japan and from rapidly industrial-
izing developing countries is providing and will continue
to provide a powerful stimulus for U.S. industry to be innovative and efficient.

SUMMARY

The standard textbook theory of the firm is more useful in a normative rather than a positive sense. Even
normatively, the usefulness of the standard theory is
somewhat limited because many of the important business
problems are concerned with a search for innovation either
in manufacturing, management, or product development, not
for optimization of known demand and production functions.
The view that corporations control the economy through
their plans, rather than the market doing so, is hard to
justify when we consider the varying degrees of corporate
success and instances of corporate failure. Finally, the
effect of potential competitors on incumbents and the implications of this for the economy is one of the most important ideas that has emerged in some time. It should be
a subject for much future research.

REFERENCES

Baumol, W. J. 1982. Contestable markets: An uprising in
    the theory of industry structure. *American Economic
    Review* 72 (March): 1-15.
Eliasson, Gunnar. 1976. *Business Economic Planning*.
    New York: Wiley.
Galbraith, John Kenneth. 1967. *The New Industrial State*.
    Boston: Houghton Mifflin.

Samuelson, Paul A. 1980. Economics. 11th ed. New
    York: McGraw-Hill.
Simon, H. A. 1959. Theories of decision making in
    economics and behaviorial science. American
    Economic Review 49 (June): 253-80.

4 *World Food Production Potential and Its Constraints*

EARL O. HEADY

    Leaders in this nation and in other countries go
through a frenzy cycle relative to world food problems.
The peak of the cycle comes when crops are poor in some
world regions, world grain prices increase dramatically,
and large groups of people suffer intensified malnutrition. The trough occurs when grain supplies are large and
domestic prices are low. We then turn away from the long-
run problems of world food supplies and human nutrition
and become more concerned, as we are now, with price sup-
ports and restrained production in the United States.
Peaks of the frenzy cycle occurred during the early 1950s
with the domestic "fifth-plate" concern, in 1966-1967 with
drought on the Indian subcontinent, and following immediately after 1972 with large crop shortfalls in Russia and
parts of Africa and Asia. By the late 1950s national concern was on land banks and other means of reducing food
supplies. Following Secretary Freeman's relaxing of supply controls in 1967, the large U.S. production and de-
pressed farm prices in 1968 possibly finalized the victory
of Nixon over Humphrey by a slight margin in the Midwest.
By 1973 we were back at the peak of the frenzy cycle a-
gain. FAO held the 1974 world food conference, and nations emphasized the production and distribution of more
food. The United States abandoned production controls in
agriculture and produced as much as it could. And by the
fall of 1977 Secretary Bergland was already proposing a
U.S. reduction by 20 percent in wheat and 10 percent in
feed grain production. Now in 1983 we have the payment in
kind (PIK) program designed to cause a vast acreage to be
removed from crop production so that supplies will be reduced and commodity prices and farm income increased. But
again, sometime in the future, weather will be bad, crop
shortfalls will occur, and we will have another transitory
world food scare.
    As long as concerns follow this oscillating and tran-

sitory pattern, sustained long-run solutions to the
world's food problems are unlikely. This cycle itself re-
strains improved world food supplies. Hence, it is useful
that we continue assessments of world food production potentials, restraints on them, and policies to attain them.

POTENTIAL SOURCES OF INCREASED PRODUCTION
     I will focus on these potentials, restraints, and
policies. It is useful first to inventory the potential
sources of increased food production and then to evaluate
the restraints. There is basis for optimism about meshing
world food supplies and demand at appropriate nutrition
levels over the next forty years if restraints on both institutions and market relationships are identified and
eliminated through appropriate policies. The picture is
still not unlike that disclosed in our basic study nearly
a decade back (Blakeslee et al. 1973). However, appropriate policies, particularly those relating to population
growth and economic incentives for producers, must be exercised effectively if the world is not to become enmeshed
in a disastrous situation from which it has no ready
escape.
     Major means of increasing world food supplies include
the following.

     1. Increasing yields through improved technologies,
such as high-yielding varieties, crop fertilization, pest
control, and improved water management, by means of research, technology transfer, and education. As explained
later, such opportunities for increasing yields are generally best in the developing countries, where current
yields are low compared with developed countries.
     2. More intensive use of currently cultivated land
through multiple cropping, intercropping, and related
means that more efficiently use available rainfall and
solar energy. There is considerable opportunity here,
especially with potential development of water supplies
and changes in water management, laws, and pricing. The
possible gains from this source have been well illustrated
in Taiwan, in the Indonesia intercropping system, and in
research at the International Rice Research Institute.
Generally, the less developed countries have climates with
long or year-round growing seasons, conforming with multiple cropping possibilities and flexibility in cropping
seasons.
     3. By bringing uncultivated land into production.

There evidently still are sizable areas in the world that
are not under crops and a considerable area devoted to
shifting cultivation. Uncultivated land prevails in considerable quantities in the savannahs of South America,
the Amazon Basin, large parts of the bush in Africa, and
the outer islands of Indonesia and Malaysia. It has been
estimated that of potentially arable land only 22 percent
in Africa, 11 percent in South America, and about 45 percent worldwide is now under cultivation (Cummings 1974;
Carter et al. 1975). The Wageningen group estimates that
whereas 1,406 million hectares currently are in cultivation, some 3,419 million hectares potentially are arable
(Buringh et al. 1975), and that irrigated land could be
increased from 200 million to 470 million hectares. Another estimate puts the world's potentially arable land at
9,000 million hectares (Clark 1970). The Food and Agriculture Organization (FAO) estimates that only half the
land that is not ice covered and could be tilled is actually in crops (Food and Agriculture Organization 1982).
While these figures are too optimistic and use of some
fragile lands could cause environmental deterioration,
land is not a scarce resource in all parts of the world.
If it were there would be less shifting cultivation. Even
the United States has a considerable amount of land that
could be brought into grain cropping under sufficient capital investment and under sustained high commodity prices.
Estimates suggest that there may be as many as 265 million
acres that could be converted to the equivalent of capability Class I-III land, with 150 million acres having
good potential for conversion (Cotner et al. 1975). (More
recently, based on the Soil Conservation Service's National Resource Inventory, this estimate has been revised to
137 million.) Capital requirements are heavy, of course,
for leveling tropical jungles, controlling second growth,
and maintaining soil fertility. Other problems of forest
soils, processing facilities, markets, and general infrastructure also prevail in some of these locations. FAO
estimates that an additional 53 million hectares of new
land could be cropped in ten years at a cost of $26 bil-
lion (at monetary values of the early 1970s) (Boerma
1975). Another 46 million hectares could be renovated
and improved for $21 billion, and irrigation schemes could
be developed on 23 million hectares for $38 billion in
ten years. These costs would be $8 billion annually over
a ten year period (under monetary values of early 1970s).
While these figures suggest feasible expansion in the

arable land base over the future, the greatest potential
for increased food production is in improved technology
and intensified production on lands already cropped.

4. By saving a greater proportion of crops that are
produced. Estimates indicate high losses, especially in
less developed countries, to rodents and birds and through
spoilage in inadequate silos and granaries.

5. By diverting a greater proportion of grains from
livestock consumption to human consumption. This is, of
course, a complex and debatable alternative (Sonka et al.
1976). In general, it implies shifting a greater proportion of the world's grain consumption from the rich countries where per capita consumption of meat is high to the
poorer countries where per capita direct consumption of
grain is high and grain consumed through livestock is low.
Since this is a controversial source of increased food
availability for the world, policies to implement it are
not likely to be initiated soon. It could, of course, be
implemented through two extremely different mechanisms.
One, an unlikely approach, would be a set of outright
rules that prevented grain feeding of livestock except in
cases where the procedure allowed a greater conversion of
waste forages or other materials into food. The second
would be through economic and market institutions. If per
capita incomes over the world suddenly could be raised to
the level of England, for example, consumers in Asia,
Africa, and South America would bid the price of grain to
be used as food so high that grain feeding of livestock
would take a drastic decline. World grain supplies would
then spread more evenly among consumers worldwide and
greater food availability from existing resources would
prevail.

6. By a greater production and utilization of foods
of sea origin. However, we may be near the limit for this
source and the future may be one of conservation rather
than expansion.

As mentioned previously, the most promising manner
for increasing food production is likely to be through
land already in cultivation. The developed market economies produce 60 percent of the world's grain production
on 36 percent of the world's grain area; the developing
countries produce only 40 percent of the world's grain
supply on the other 64 percent of the area (Rojko et al.
1978). If land productivity in the less developed countries were pushed to the level of the developed countries,

world food production would increase 67 percent. The capability of the world to produce more food also is apparent from the yield trends in developed and developing countries. In the period 1934-1938, grain yields averaged 1.15 tons per hectare in developed countries and 1.14 tons in developing countries--practically the same yield. In the period 1973-1975, yields in the developed countries averaged 3.0 tons, in the developing countries 1.4 tons (International Food Policy Research Institute 1977). Of the industrialized countries, only Japan had a significant increase in grain yields in the nineteenth century. In the last twenty-five years of that century, Japanese grain yields increased from 1.3 tons to 1.9 tons per hectare. Otherwise, most of the yield increase in industrialized countries has occurred in the last forty years. Before 1940, grain yields in the United States averaged less than 1.5 tons per hectare but in recent years have been 3.5 tons. There is little reason why developing countries cannot do as well or better than developed countries, particularly since the former are largely in tropical climates, with multiple-cropping opportunities, while the latter are mostly in temperate climates.

In the 1930s only a small amount of chemical technology was used in the agriculture of both developing and developed countries. Improvement in varieties and use of hybrids was modest everywhere, compared with developments since then. An important reason for differences in yield trends has been investment in agricultural research and education. This was the basis for the early Japanese gain in land productivity (Hayami and Ruttan 1971), and especially for the United States in the last four decades.

Although their populations are the most threatened with future food shortages, the developing countries tend to undervalue agriculture. This attitude is reflected in their overly modest investments in agricultural research and in their allocation of the major share of development investment to other industries. It is also reflected in their pricing policies, which use many methods to depress prices to farmers for the benefit of consumers. The Thailand export tax on rice drives down farm prices to lower the retail prices for urban consumers. Estimations suggest that during recent decades rice has been underpriced, relative to world markets by as much as 50 percent in India (Sukhatme 1976). Controlled cereal prices in Egypt have caused farmers to shift resources to meat, vegetables, and other commodities lacking controls. Other Asian

and African countries similarly have used pricing policies
and marketing boards to keep real prices of farm commodities low. Simultaneously, many of them keep the prices
of fertilizers at high real levels. The United States has
contributed to this distortion of prices and restraint of
agricultural improvement. Hertford et al. (1977) show
that between 1953 and 1973, during a period of large imports of low-cost P.L. 480 grain from the United States,
wheat acreage in Colombia fell sharply and investment in
wheat research was cut by one-half. Perhaps the stage is
being set to do so again. Above-market support prices in
the United States, without completely effective supply
controls in sight, will lead, as in the 1950s, to an accumulation of large stocks. We then will be likely to export our surplus problem as food aid, which again would
drive down the prices cultivators receive in developing
countries.

Developing countries have undervalued agriculture to
emphasize the industrial and consumer sectors, which are
better organized, more vocal, and/or have a greater political strength. But some developed countries have over-
valued and overpriced agriculture. Of the many examples,
the Common Market countries and Japan stand out and the
United States is moving in this direction again. By pricing policies and import levies imports are blocked from
countries that can produce more and at lower cost than
they are now producing. Trade with developing countries
is thus discouraged. While developing countries do import
some food, agriculture is a major source of exports. In
many developing countries as much as 50 percent of foreign
exchange earnings come from agricultural exports. So
trade policies, as well as domestic price policies and an
undervaluing of agriculture, obstruct the movement of poor
countries toward their full food-producing potential.

With yields on cereal acreage in the developing countries less than half those on an equal acreage in developed nations, the physical potential for increasing world
food supplies is quite obvious. Water resources now used
for irrigation over much of the developing world are de-
ployed inefficiently. Improving the physical, legal, and
economic conditions surrounding water use could mean a
considerable increment to food supplies, as could the further development of water resources. Land reclamation to
bring a great area under cultivation could do much to increase food supplies. How much it should do depends on
the supply price that the world's consumers are willing to

pay for food and the trade-offs implied in producing more
food for more people at the expense of other investment
alternatives on behalf of humanity. Certainly much food
could be produced on land not now cropped if humanity
could make the needed investments and drive the supply
price of food high enough. This will probably happen if
per capita incomes and population in the developing countries increase sufficiently and simultaneously. Under
certain conditions of growth, however, developing countries are going to have to face more directly the trade-
off among major competing alternatives such as (1) continued rapid population growth, investment in land reclamation, and high marginal supply prices for food or (2)
reduced population growth and greater investment in education, housing, and health facilities.

AGGREGATE PRODUCTION POSSIBILITIES
     A number of studies have projected world food produc-
tion into the future. The Wageningen group is highly optimistic for the long run, estimating the absolute maximum
potential food production to be almost 40 times greater
than that of current production (Buringh et al. 1975).
Our own projections, while less optimistic, also suggest
favorable possibilities for the next thirty years, a period in which the developing countries could begin to get
their house in order by reducing population growth rates
(Blakeslee et al. 1973). FAO estimates that food production could increase by 3.7 percent per year to year 2000,
with 14 percent coming from greater land area, 16 percent
from crop intensification, and 70 percent from improved
technology (Food and Agriculture Organization 1982).
     Not all estimates of future supply-demand balances
are so optimistic. The Club of Rome presented a dark outlook with any scenario (Mesarovic and Pestal 1974). The
estimates of the International Food Policy Research Institute (1977) for developing market economy countries alone
indicated a 10 percent gap between production and "needed
food consumption" within these countries in 1990 if per
capita consumption levels remain at 1975 levels. In 1990
the gap between production and demand within these countries, with income growth at high levels, is estimated to
be 21 percent.

RESTRAINTS IN ATTAINING PRODUCTION POTENTIAL
     To be optimistic with respect to how much food can be

produced is not being optimistic with respect to how much
will be produced. How much will be produced from available arable land and water resources depends on the implementation of appropriate policies that influence food production in the developing countries. To a large extent,
augmentation of their food supplies does not involve new
or mysterious processes. It requires processes that are
already known in executing agricultural research, in in-
vesting in land and improved water development, in keeping
agricultural production profitable, in augmenting input
supplies, and in related steps. But administrators and
politicians in developing countries must be serious about
applying appropriate policies so that these processes are
implemented.

The task of selecting and implementing appropriate
policies should be easier in the future. Some important
progress has been made in recent decades. Over the period
1960-1975, cereal production in the developing countries
increased at the rate of 3 percent per year, considerably
above the population rate of 2.5 percent. In the period
1960-1966, some 56 percent of the increase came from expansion of land area; during 1967-1975, nearly 70 percent
came from increases in yield. With the potentials summarized earlier, it would seem that as much or more could
be accomplished in the next two decades. Developing countries are better supplied with trained and experienced
manpower and administrators than they were in the last
three decades, when most were only a few years removed
from colonial administration.

To be optimistic about the ability of the world to
produce enough food to keep up with population increases
and eliminate a good share of existing malnutrition over
the next thirty years does not solve the longer run problem of high birth rates and population growth over the
next hundred years. But the world does have a period of
thirty or forty years in which to gear up programs to reduce birth rates. The variables involved are complex, and
they must be tackled with greater vigor immediately if
population and food demand are to be reasonably restrained
against food supplies in the long run. They include not
only the conventional educational and technical means for
reducing birth rates but also increased per capita income,
improving the worth of women's time, and developing social
security or old-age pension programs. Data from less developed countries indicate elasticity of births with respect to income and education of women to be -.33 and
-.25, respectively, compared with +.25 for education of

men. An improvement in the value of women's time through
education, employment opportunities, and economic and social participation is a necessary step in reducing birth
rates. The opportunity cost of a woman's time must become
so great that she cannot afford to produce so many children. Similarly, social security programs must be developed in all countries in order that parents do not have to
raise many children to support them in old age.

During the thirty or forty years that developing
countries have available to attain these conditions on the
side of population and demand, physical restraints are not
likely to serve as the ultimate limits on food supplies.
The binding restraints are more nearly those of economic
policies that prevent available physical resources from
being sufficiently developed, depress incentives to use
more purchased inputs, and interfere with trade that would
better exploit international comparative advantages in
food production.

Investments in Research, Communication, and Personnel

The earlier Japanese advances and the yield gains of
the United States over recent decades resulted from investments in research the results of which were then com-
municated effectively to farmers. In earlier times this
investment in research was made mainly by the public. In
recent times, as agriculture has become more capitalized,
the private sector has been equally important in research-
ing and communicating new production possibilities to
farmers. In developing countries, however, this investment remains largely a function of government enterprise.

An increase in expenditures on agricultural research
is necessary if the production potential on presently cultivated lands is to be attained. The gap cannot be completely filled by the international research institutes
funded by donor nations, since much adaptive research is
site specific. The low-income countries invest only 25-40
percent as much on research, relative to the value of production, as do the developed, high-income countries (Boyce
and Evenson 1975). The international institutes can contribute greatly in more basic work, such as developing
genetic materials. While providing a foundation for further improvement, developments such as these do not substitute for the adaptive research and the development of
practices that are complementary with the local environment. Also, there is a possibility that existence of the
international centers may lead developing countries to

rely too heavily on them and neglect their own national
research programs.

Research restraints stem not only from the magnitude
of investments. Related problems are those of the organization of research and the supply of trained personnel
and salary levels. While a few developing countries have
a fairly large number of persons trained to the Ph.D.
level, lack of trained manpower is the dominating restraint in most. It is, of course, a restraint that can
be overcome in the next decade if developing and donor
countries are willing to make the investment. As many as
30,000 university graduates per year are required for an
agricultural research and extension system sufficient to
promote agricultural development at a reasonable rate.
But if such an investment is made, research institutes
must still be able to hold newly trained personnel. In
the majority of developing countries salary levels in research institutes and universities are too low to attract
young scientists. Other problems of research organization
exist, such as seniority and bureaucratic systems that
discourage newly trained personnel and the concentration
of research on one or two major cereals and/or industrial
crops, with little emphasis on root, protein, and similar
foods.

Hopefully, the supply of manpower, compared with two
decades ago, is now large enough that a good number of developing countries can begin to pursue aggressive agricultural research programs. A situation that should have
spurred them to do so was the relative shortage and high
price of food during the mid-1970s. There is little evidence, however, that any quantum leaps were made in the
magnitude of investment or the organization of agricultural research.

Pricing Policies

As mentioned previously, national pricing policies
have served as one restraint on cultivator investments and
greater food supplies. Much has been learned about the
responsiveness to price of cultivators in developing countries over the last two decades (Timmer and Falcon 1975).
That even illiterate operators with small farms respond
positively to favorable commodity-input price ratios is
well quantified. Policymakers and administrators may
heed this information and refrain in the future from programs that cause farm commodities to be undervalued and
inputs to be overpriced. There is some indication that a

number of countries that underpriced agricultural commodities in the past have moved toward more useful pricing
policies. At best, a combination of economic evidence of
the past and better trained and experienced policy administrators will provide pricing regimes to spur agricultural improvement in the developing countries. Input subsidies, which in the past have had a record mainly of
bringing gain to larger farmers, can be used to provide an
initial push toward adoption of new technologies by both
large and small farmers.

International Policies and Trade

International programs that cause farm commodities to
be underpriced are an extension of domestic policies with
a similar effect. One program in this category is the
limitation of exports until domestic consumption needs are
met. As mentioned previously, the United States partici-
pated in depressing prices in developing countries through
its massive P.L. 480 food aid program, the dominant purpose of which was to improve domestic prices by moving
surplus supplies out of U.S. markets. While producers in
developing countries have had a respite from U.S. surplus
disposal programs in recent years, the current complaint
over commodity surpluses and the farmer press for parity
could again cause U.S. farm commodities to be overpriced,
the accumulation of large stocks, and the implementation
of an international food aid program to relieve domestic
markets. Ongoing developments in the United States close-
ly parallel those of the 1950s and 1960s, which gave rise
to mammoth exports under public assistance.

Indirectly, too, all policies that dampen trade of
developed countries with developing countries restrain development of the latter. An important limitation in most
developing countries is foreign exchange. Whether lack of
foreign exchange directly limits capital goods imports for
industrial or agricultural uses, the effect is generally
to restrain development. Some improvements for agriculture depend directly on imported capital goods and technology, such as improved seeds or fertilizers. In other
cases, if foreign exchange is not available for industrial
goods, more of the domestic budget may be shifted from
agriculture to the industrial sector.

Capital and Manpower Restraints

While perhaps not dominant, limited capital also is a
restraint to the further development of world food supplies. It especially serves as a restraint in adoption of

improved technology by small cultivators. It need not do
so in the long run, however, if credit policies are
adapted to serve this strata of farmers as they do the
larger farmers in developing countries.

Capital is a major restraint in the clearing and
leveling of land, in improving water distribution, and developing new, large irrigation systems. In large areas
that might be reclaimed for crops, sizable investment in
roads and infrastructure would be necessary. In many
cases lack of public investment restricts private investment in land reclamation. Lack of profitability or price
instability may be a major restraint to reclaiming the remaining land area that could be converted to crops. A
large amount of this land will be brought into cultivation
when per capita incomes and food demand drive prices to
sufficiently high levels for a sustained period of time.
United States farmers had 13 percent more land in crop
production in 1982 than in 1972. Had soybeans remained at
$12 and corn and wheat at $5 for a decade (their prices in
1973), farmers would have plowed up and cropped many more
of the 135-265 million acres of potential Class I-II cropland. Hence, the constraint on this conversion might be
considered to be price level, with equal application to
other countries. With grains at their 1973-1975 real
level for thirty years, great quantities of soybeans would
be flushed out of Brazil from land not now in crops. Similar developments would take place in cereal and palm oil
production elsewhere in the world.

It is possible that capital availability has been
less a restraint on agricultural productivity than the al-
locative patterns used for its investment. Only about 10
percent of international aid funds have gone into agriculture, while a disproportionate amount has gone into industry and perhaps even into some aspects of education. Some
claim that even the capital allotted to agriculture has
been misallocated, especially for capital intensive land
infrastructure development (Barker 1977).

Although it is not readily quantified, management is
considered to have been a more binding constraint than
capital in limiting the rate and extent of agricultural
development in the past. The lack of sufficiently able
and experienced management personnel leads to inappropriate allocation of capital investment and inefficient execution of initiated projects. Common examples are large-
scale public irrigation investments that lack efficient
tertiary canals and water distribution systems, ineffec-
tive extension services, and input distributing facilities

that stand still. This restraint need not, of course, prevail in the long run. Most developing countries have more trained personnel than in the 1950s. And further investments in human capital for these purposes can and should be made, since the problem is currently crucial in some countries.

Environmental Restraints

Reference has been made to the world's potential arable land. Much of it is not now cropped because of unfavorable environmental conditions, including limited moisture and soil deficiencies. Before the very large areas projected by Clark (1970) and Buringh et al. (1975) could be fully converted to cropland, land would need to come from pasture, forests, and jungle. Some of these lands are in fragile environments.

Environmental conditions will restrain cultivation and intensive grazing of lands until conditions and technologies are found that can remove the negative environmental impacts. These conditions may require international management and allocation of water and grazing, partic-. ularly diversion and control of water at river headwaters.

Water Management

While the FAO estimates indicate another 23 million hectares of land could feasibly be irrigated by 1985, perhaps equally important in food potential is improved water management systems for land already under irrigation. In all countries historic rights, customs, politics, and cultural conditions are barriers to water allocation based on its value of marginal productivity. Even in the United States, greater production could be forthcoming from given surface supplies if water allocation was broken from its pattern of historic rights and was allowed to move where its marginal productivity is greatest. Existing conditions surrounding water use cause investments in distribution systems to be minimized. Farmers at the head of main canals receive too much water, those at the end too little. Supplies are certain for some and undependable for others. Even international development agencies invest in systems with sufficient primary and secondary canals but with inefficient tertiary canals and on-farm distribution systems.

ULTIMATE RESTRAINT

The restraints on world food production are not in-

surmountable. Prospects for the future are positive.
And, at least in the intermediate future, restraints of
social and economic policies are more important than physical restraints. Attaining the possibilities of food production will require political stability and wise economic
and social policies. These policies must provide economic
incentives both for exploiting physical resources and for
checking population growth.

REFERENCES

Barker, Randolph. 1977. Barriers to efficient capital
    investment in agriculture. Paper presented at work-
    shop on resources, incentives, and agriculture,
    University of Chicago.
Blakeslee, Leroy L., Earl O. Heady, and Charles F.
    Framingham. 1973. World Food Production, Demand
    and Trade. Ames: Iowa State University Press.
Boerma, A. H. 1975. The world could be fed. Journal
    of Soil and Water Conservation 30(1):4-11.
Boyce, J., and R. E. Evenson. 1975. Agricultural
    Research and Extension Programs. New York: Agri-
    cultural Development Council.
Buringh, P., H. P. J. van Heemst, and G. J. Staring.
    1975. The absolute maximum food production of the
    world. Paper presented the third IIASA Symposium
    on Global Modeling: Food and Agriculture, Project
    on Food for a Doubling World Population, Free
    University, Amsterdam.
Carter, Harold O., James G. Youde, and Maurice L. Peter-
    son. 1975. Future land requirements to produce food
    for an expanding world population. In Perspectives
    on Prime Lands, Seminar on Retention of Prime
    Lands. Washington, D.C.: USDA.
Clark, Colin. 1970. Population and Agricultural Growth
    Change in Agriculture. London: Duckworth.
Cotner, M. L., M. D. Skold, and Orville Krause. 1975.
    Farmland: Will there be enough? ERS 584, Economic
    Research Service, USDA.
Cummings, Ralph W., Jr. 1974. Food production and the
    energy crisis. Working Papers of the Rockefeller
    Foundation, New York.
Food and Agriculture Organization. 1982. Agriculture:
    Toward 2000. Rome.
Hayami, Yujiro, and Vernon Ruttan. 1971. Agricultural
    Development: An International Perspective.

Baltimore: The Johns Hopkins University Press.
Hertford, Reed, Jorge Ardila, Andres Roches, and Carlos
    Trujillo. 1977. Productivity of agricultural re-
    search in Colombia. In Resource Allocation and
    Productivity in National and Interregional Agri-
    cultural Research, ed. Thomas M. Arndt et al.
    Minneapolis: University of Minnesota Press.
International Food Policy Research Institute. 1977. Food
    needs of developing countries: Projections of pro-
    duction and consumption to 1990. Washington, D.C.
Johnson, D. Gale. 1977. Food production potential in
    Southeast Asia and other developing countries. Paper
    77:19, Office of Agricultural Economics Research,
    University of Chicago.
Mesarovic, Mihajlo, and Edward Pestal. 1974. Mankind at
    the Turning Point: The Second Report to the Club of
    Rome. New York, Dutton.
Rojko, Anthony, et al. 1978. Alternative Futures for
    World Food Production in 1985. World GOL Model
    Analytical Report, vol. 1. Foreign Economic Report
    146. Washington, D.C.: USDA, Economics, Statistics,
    and Cooperatives Service.
Sonka, Steven T., Earl O. Heady, and Doeke C. Faber.
    1976. Human and Veterinary Nutrition. U.S.
    Nutrition and Dietetics, vol. 26, no. 1.
Sukhatme, V.A. 1976. The utilization of high yielding
    rice and wheat varieties in India: An economic
    assessment. Ph.D. diss. University of Chicago.
Timmer, C. Peter, and W. P. Falcon. 1975. The political
    economy of rice production in East Asia. In Agricul-
    tural Development Theory, ed. Lloyd G. Reynolds.
    New Haven: Yale University Press.

5   *Ethics, Economics, and the Environment*

ROBERT DORFMAN

The Environmental Protection Agency (EPA) was very much in the news in 1983 because of widespread charges of favoritism in administering funds, of paper shredders where they shouldn't be, of laxity in supervising the disposal of toxic wastes, and assorted other misconduct. A chapter about these and other juicy scandals at EPA would be pleasanter than this one because it is always more agreeable to consider other people's lax moral standards than to scrutinize our own. Nevertheless, I plan to discuss not the EPA's but the public's moral standards and how they have contributed to confusion and ineffectiveness in the national effort to protect and improve the environment.

It has been said, probably too often, that a nation gets the government it deserves. Whether that is true, the characteristics of a nation do have a profound and far-reaching effect on its government. When I look at our attempts to attain a safe and pleasant environment in this country, I am appalled at how indecisive, confused, and wasteful they have been, and I try to understand why. There is never a single, simple explanation of a complicated social state of affairs. It is altogether too easy when contemplating unsatisfactory social performance to say that some people wear white hats and some wear black, that the mean and selfish people in the black hats are frustrating the noble ones in white for their own nefarious purposes. In other words, somebody else's morals are at fault. I reject that easy kind of explanation. On the contrary, I look for an explanation grounded in the nature of the problem.

The government's environmental programs, like all its programs, are responses to public pressures and demands.

65

In the case of environmental protection, we have been demanding two contradictory things, and whenever the government attempts to provide one of them, the contrary goal interferes. Hence the indecisiveness and confusion. I will try to clarify that thought, give a few instances of the interplay between contradictory demands in the environmental area, and discuss how those demands can be reconciled (to the extent they can be).

The contradictory demands arise from two conflicting ethical principles deeply embedded in the American tradition: the doctrine of natural rights and utilitarianism. It is not a case of some people adhering to one ethical principle and other people adhering to the other one. I, for one, believe in both, and I think that most people do, and since these principles are contradictory, they confuse us.

THE DOCTRINE OF NATURAL RIGHTS

The doctrine of natural rights (and of its close relative, natural laws) goes back at least to Roman times. Given its most influential modern formulation by John Locke in seventeenth century England, it states that every man has certain inherent, inviolable rights that cannot legitimately be invaded and that the actions of every government are circumscribed by certain natural laws that it cannot legitimately violate. This doctrine was influential in America from the very beginning, such as justifying the Declaration of Independence: "We hold these truths to be self-evident, that all men are created equal, that they are endowed by their Creator with certain inalienable rights, and that among these are life, liberty, and the pursuit of happiness. . . ." It was incorporated in the U.S. Constitution most expressly in the Bill of Rights and later in the Fourteenth Amendment and has been reiterated countless times since. And these are not merely empty words; we believe them and many of our laws are intended to implement them.

Since we all share this system of beliefs we should all be aware that it has some shortcomings. There is no generally agreed on list of the rights that are held to be inalienable and no guidance about what should be done when one of those rights conflicts with another one or when the rights of one individual conflict with the rights of others. Rights and wrongs are complicated things, and we should not expect any clear and simple principle to resolve all issues.

I have cited ancient sources and inarticulate
feelings. But I want to remind you that there are elo-
quent spokesmen for this doctrine today. Milton Friedman
(1982), Robert Nozick (1981), and the whole libertarian
school argue effectively that it is wrong for a government
to invade any citizen's natural rights for the benefit of
other citizens. Of course, all governments do that habit-
ually, as when they implement various welfare programs,
and it is against such practices that the libertarians
levy their diatribes.

As mentioned earlier, there is no accepted catalog of
natural rights. In particular, the usual list makes no
explicit mention of the environment. But it does include
the right of every person that his life and health not be
sacrificed or endangered for the benefit of others. Releasing harmful pollutants into the environment falls under these bans, and most of our environmental regulations
are intended to protect those natural rights. Furthermore
(but I am not sure of this) the doctrine of natural law
may enjoin every nation to preserve its environment and to
keep the creatures in it in a healthy state. The preamble
to the Clean Water Act appears to accept this responsibility. It reads, "The objective of the Act is to restore
and maintain the chemical, physical, and biological integ-
rity of the nation's waters. In order to achieve this
objective it is hereby declared that consistent with the
provisions of the Act it is the national goal that the
discharge of pollutants into the navigable waters be eliminated by 1985." In short, the doctrine of natural rights
is deeply embedded in the American tradition, and Amer-
icans look to their government to help effect those rights
in the environmental sphere as well as elsewhere.

UTILITARIANISM

Utilitarianism is equally deeply embedded in the
American tradition. The word was coined in the nineteenth
century, but the idea was prominent even in Epicurean phi-
losophy, and Socrates espoused it in at least one of the
dialogues. The central thrust is conveyed by the eigh-
teenth century expression, "the greatest good for the
greatest number." Taken literally the words don't make
much sense, but the main idea does. It holds that the
sole criterion of whether a government should undertake
any action is the effect of that action on the public welfare, somehow defined. According to utilitarian principles it is right and proper for a government to undertake

any action that enhances public welfare and correspondingly wrong and improper for it to refrain from such an
action or to undertake one that reduces public welfare.
Notice that this doctrine is in flagrant contradiction to
the natural rights ethic. Natural rights holds that at
least some actions are inherently right or wrong, regardless of their consequences; utilitarianism holds that the
rightness or wrongness of an action depends only on its
consequences.

In the United States, utilitarianism was enunciated
in the preamble to the Constitution, as one of the purposes of the new government was stated to be promoting the
general welfare. Further on in the Constitution, providing for the general welfare of the United States was specifically included among the powers of Congress. That power was put to work almost immediately in Alexander Hamil-
ton's "Report on Manufactures" and has been exercised ever
since. Skipping over more than a hundred years, the utilitarian foundation of the general welfare concept was af-
firmed in a passage that is especially dear to my heart
and that has had widespread consequences. In the Water
Resources Act of 1936 the Corps of Engineers was instructed to build reservoirs or other improvements only if "the
benefits exceed the costs to whomsoever they may accrue."
This is out-and-out utilitarianism, and naive utilitarianism at that. The same concept has been repeated many
times since, most recently in an order by President Reagan
requiring all agencies of the federal government to estimate and take account of the benefits and costs of the decisions that they propose.

The definition of the general welfare formulated in
the Water Resources Act has been a powerful precedent and
has influenced both congressional and executive decisions
ever since. Under its influence, the conscious weighing
of costs and benefits has become such a conspicuous feature of government decision making in Congress and agencies that we all regard it simply as common sense. A whole
discipline has grown up composed of people who are skilled, or at least specialized, in making such estimates and
who have developed a substantial literature.

The assertion that there is a fundamental contradiction between the natural rights tradition, with its emphasis on inherent rightness and wrongness, and the utilitarian tradition, with its emphasis on results, has been
questioned. A redoubtable opponent, John Stuart Mill
(1963), argued that natural rights are derivative from the
utilitarian ethic because everyone recognizes that

whenever anyone's natural rights are violated, everyone's
life, liberty and security of property are endangered and
the general welfare is severely diminished. If the utilitarian tradition is so construed the conflict is resolv-
ed, at least verbally. But then it ceases to be an applicable standard for any practical purpose. When Congress
instructed the Corps of Engineers to take account of the
benefits and costs to whomever they may accrue, they
clearly did not expect the Corps to estimate the feelings
of insecurity that might be generated when any piece of
property is condemned; in fact, such considerations never
do enter official estimates of benefits and costs, though
they are sometimes raised in the course of public debate.
I do not maintain that any utilitarian--and I am one, as
well as a believer in natural rights--has thought through
such subtleties. If we had there might be no confusion.
I do maintain that when the Congress instructed the Corps
of Engineers to take account of benefits and costs, the
Congress was speaking in the main line of the utilitarian
tradition and intended the Corps to compare concrete, observable benefits to some people with concrete, observable
costs to others. The general welfare would be considered
served if the benefits outweighed the costs. It is implicit in this approach that when the stated criterion is
applied consistently some people will be helped and some
harmed on each occasion, but on balance everyone will be
helped more than harmed. Therefore this rule unambiguous-
ly promotes the general welfare by promoting the welfare
of each member of the community. Subtle considerations
such as the one advanced by Mill have no place in it.
President Reagan's order (and a similar presidential order
by his predecessor, President Carter) were clearly intended in the same pragmatic spirit and have been obeyed in
that spirit.

THREE ILLUSTRATIONS OF CONFLICTING GOALS
        Thus we have inherited a pair of conflicting ethical
principles, to both of which we are deeply committed. In
our environmental affairs, as elsewhere, we try to implement both of them. The result, inevitably, is confusion.
EPA, which bears the major responsibility for administering environmental laws, is instructed to move in two different directions at the same time, which it cannot do.
How it manages to live with such instructions is an interesting story. Following are three brief illustrations of
the agency's struggle to contend, one from the Clean Water
Act, one from the Clean Air Act, and one from the Toxic

Substances Control Act, all of which in different ways
direct EPA to regulate intrusions on the environment so as
to prevent violations of citizens' rights and simultaneously promote the general welfare.

The Clean Water Act

    The inspiring statement of objectives with which the
Clean Water Act begins has already been quoted. It af-
firms that the national goal is to eliminate the discharge
of all pollutants into navigable waters by 1985. In 1983,
as far as acts of Congress are concerned, that was still
the national goal. Needless to say, there is no possibility of achieving it, and I cannot believe that any of the
senators and representatives who voted for that act were
naive enough to believe polluting discharges could be
eliminated completely in thirteen years, if ever. They
voted for it nevertheless, enough of them to override a
presidential veto, because that was the year of the presidential election that immediatley followed Earth Day
(1972) and public concern about the state of the environment was at its height. Congress heard a loud public demand that the waters be cleaned up; and without too much
niggling over the wording of the act, it passed, was ve-
toed, and three weeks before the election passed again.
Congress does listen.

    The goals are just words, of course, but words writ-
ten into law have consequences. The consequence of these
words is that the EPA could not, and cannot, direct its
effort toward cleaning up the lakes and rivers where the
pollution is most damaging. Instead it must implement a
program called the National Pollution Elimination System,
which attempts to reduce discharges of pollutants everywhere, whether damaging or not. Even without further com-
plication this compels the agency to squander billions of
dollars (from a utilitarian point of view), for example,
in financing the construction of waste treatment plants in
places where natural processes would purify the water before anyone was inconvenienced.

    There are further complications. Utilitarian consid-
erations were not forgotten in writing the body of the
act. It was clear that restricting polluting discharges
--not to mention eliminating them--would impose heavy
costs on food-processing plants, steel mills, and many
other industries that use large amounts of water and
return it, polluted, to lakes and rivers. The law, therefore, imposes restrictions on what EPA can order such
plants to do. A five-year transition period was allowed,

after which EPA could (and should) require all plants in
the country to reduce their polluting discharges by the
amount achievable by applying "the best practicable control technology currently available." Beginning in 1983
EPA was told to require "the best available technology
economically achievable." Congress was careful not to
define those words in the act, leaving that delicate task
to EPA. EPA has given definitions and has changed them
several times, always with careful attention to the quali-
fication "economically achievable," which it enforced in
such a way that none but the most marginal plants could be
rendered unprofitable by the clean-up requirements.

Needless to say, the enforcement of this restriction
left room for a great deal of pollution. Unintentionally
another large loophole was left. Farms generate a vast a-
mount of pollution; unless precautions are taken, rains
wash fertilizers and pesticide residues into nearby lakes
and streams. The animal wastes generated on livestock
feedlots also end up in public waters in large quantities.
EPA was not given any authority to control those sources
of pollution.

In these and other ways the text of the act undercut
thoroughly the announced objective but still did not allow
EPA to undertake the measures needed to reduce water pollution in proportion to the damage it caused. Neither the
natural rights nor the utilitarian objective was served.

The Clean Air Act

In one of the major provisions of the Clean Air Act
the shoe is on the other foot. The announced purpose of
the act, "to protect and enhance the quality of the nation's air resources so as to promote the public health
and welfare and the productive capacity of its population," is as utilitarian as anybody could want, but the
operating provisions go the other way. In particular they
require EPA to establish and enforce requirements (called
national primary ambient air quality standards) defined as
"ambient air quality standards the attainment and maintenance of which in the judgment of the administrator and
allowing an adequate margin of safety are requisite to
protect the public health." This sounds like a perfectly
reasonable and humane provision, but it contains at least
three pitfalls that have caused unending difficulty since
the law was enacted.

The first pitfall was the Senate's explanation of
what they meant by "protecting the public health." They
meant protecting the health of all persons exposed to

outdoor air, including--and the example is the Senate's--
persons who suffer from emphysema. So EPA was instructed
to identify the population group that was most vulnerable
to the effects of any air pollutant and to set a standard
strict enough to protect them though they might be a few
in number. A standard set in accordance with this criterion would inevitably be much stricter, and correspondingly
more expensive to attain, than one that would suffice to
protect the great bulk of the population.

That requirement might not have caused so much trou-
ble except for the other two pitfalls. The second one is
scientific. The law, as interpreted by the Senate, pre-
sumes that there is some level of a pollutant in the air
that will do no harm to even the most sensitive individuals. Whether there is any such level is a scientific
question; epidemiologists and toxicologists refer to it as
the question of the existence of a threshold. No source
that I have consulted answers that question with great
confidence, but the weight of opinion with respect to most
air pollutants is that there is no threshold below which a
pollutant does no harm to anyone. If there is no such
threshold, EPA would have to require that all man-made
discharges of pollution be stopped--exactly the same unat-
tainable level of aspiration encountered when discussing
the Clean Water Act.

The third pitfall is one that, so far as I know, is
unique to the air quality provisions of this act. The requirement that the air quality standards should be strict
enough to protect the health of all individuals makes no
mention of costs, and there is no qualifying provision
that permits EPA to take costs into account in establishing air quality standards. Taken literally, this in-
structs EPA to pay no heed to costs in setting standards
strict enough to protect the most susceptible person in
the population. This might well require forbidding all
emissions of some pollutants. It surely conflicts with
the announced purpose of promoting public welfare and the
productive capacity of the population.

Naturally, EPA has done no such thing. Instead it
has assumed that for every pollutant there is a threshold
concentration below which no one would be harmed, despite
the weight of scientific opinion. The agency has established the threshold at a level that is attainable in
practice and at the same time appears not to harm susceptible individuals noticeably more than a lower practical
level, being careful, all the while, not to mention costs.

My favorite example is carbon monoxide (CO). The current standard permits 9 parts CO per million parts air. Now it happens that there is no evidence that CO at that level of concentration or anywhere near it harms anybody except people who suffer from severe angina pectoris. They are few in number and, besides, it doesn't affect them much. The situation is that an angina patient has a very marginal supply of oxygen to the heart muscle. Anything that increases the heart's need for oxygen, such as exercise, can bring on a terribly painful attack. The CO in the air reduces the blood's ability to supply oxygen. The result is that if an angina patient engages in exercise that would bring on an attack in 3 minutes in pure air, the attack will be induced in about 2 1/2 minutes if the air contains 10 to 12 parts per million CO. There are no aftereffects. The ambient standard for CO has been set primarily with this effect in mind and is low enough so that stricter but still attainable standards would not noticeably reduce the amount of exercise the patient could take before experiencing an attack.

No one knows how much money could be saved without significant harm by relaxing this standard or others set by similar considerations, because EPA is not allowed to look into that. My impression is that it is substantial.

Of course, these strict standards are not met universally. The latest data I have show that in 1978 the CO standard was violated on ten or more days in more than half the communities in New England, the Pacific Northwest, and the Mountain States, and by large proportions in nearly all parts of the country.

In short, in the case of the Clean Air Act, the public gave mixed signals and EPA received confusing instructions. It was told to "promote public health and welfare," but to pay no attention to the effects on the general welfare when setting the national ambient air quality standards. Air quality in most cities has improved, but the drain on other aspects of general welfare, as measured by the dollar cost, has been enormous--about $25 billion a year. Much of the drain was probably unnecessary.

The Toxic Substances Control Act

The final example concerns a currently notorious function of EPA: regulation of the use and disposal of toxic substances. No law is proof against malfeasance and nonfeasance, though a law can facilitate those things by being confused and indecisive. The current furor over toxic substances concerns their proper final interment; this example deals with the other end of their biography, their creation. That aspect of control may some day be in the news because the provisions of the act that regulate the introduction of new toxic substances have not been implemented seven years after their enactment.

To understand this seven years of effective paralysis, we have to look at the act itself and its context. Though the Toxic Substances Control Act was passed in 1976, it was conceived about six years earlier, at the crest of the wave of environmental awareness. People were frightened, and properly frightened, at the dangerousness of injecting new and untried substances into their environment, homes, diets—everywhere. The ingenuity of chemists is vast. Roughly a thousand new chemicals are invented and introduced commercially every year. Nearly all are harmless, maybe 990 out of 1,000, but a few—such as dioxin—are terrible. The problem is how to detect in time the handful of dangerous ones without shutting off the flow of beneficial ones.

Congress wrestled with this problem for about six years before emerging with a program known as Premanufacturing Notification. It requires everyone who wishes to introduce a new chemical into the United States to inform EPA in advance and to provide enough information about it so that the agency can judge whether to permit it, to permit it under certain restrictions, or to forbid it. And that is where the blockage, extending for six years before enactment and since then, arose. Just what informtion should the prospective manufacturers and importers be required to provide?

Providing information about hazards is expensive. Moderately thorough testing of a new chemical for carcinogenicity and mutagenicity takes two years and costs from a half million to a million dollars. To demand such tests for all new substances—about most of which there are no grounds for suspicion—would stop chemical innovation in its tracks. Besides, chemical innovators are normally very reluctant to divulge information about their new products that would be likely to give valuable clues to their competitiors.

So some compromise with the goal of absolute protection is necessary if the chemical industry is to survive. The Congress wrestled long and hard with this problem, and in the end fudged it. It set forth rather vague requirements for information and gave EPA the power to require more information if it had good grounds for doing so. In addition, it inserted numerous safeguards into the act to prevent EPA from making onerous demands when they were not necessary. For example, EPA must demonstrate its need for anything beyond such minimal information as the name and chemical formula of the new substance; a manufacturer not satisfied with EPA's demonstration may appeal to the courts for permission to proceed without providing the data requested.

So the act contains an internal tension. On the one hand, EPA has the responsibility for regulating the introduction of new toxic substances; on the other, it was left with the task of determining specifically what information it needs in order to discharge that responsibility and its authority to require information was severely restricted. And, to cut short a long and discouraging story, from that day on, EPA has not been able to propose a schedule of information to be provided that the chemical manufacturers would accept. In the absence of such a schedule, manufacturers just give EPA the information about new products that they think proper and EPA makes do with it. The result is just what you would expect. About 60 percent of the notifications received contain no data on safety testing, and the data in the rest tend to be skimpy. No one regards this as a satisfactory state of affairs, so the effort to devise a useful set of information requirements acceptable to the manufacturers continues.

The interplay of ethical and other considerations in the case of this act is more intricate than in the preceding two. Remember that the toxic substances act was conceived at the peak of the zeal for environmental protection, in an assertion of the public's right to be safe from harmful chemicals. There was also a utilitarian tinge, since the sickness, suffering, and property loss that toxic chemicals can cause are catastrophic reductions in the welfare of the victims (as the Love Canal and Times Beach episodes remind us). On the utilitarian side, there was a concern to retain the benefits the many new synthetics confer on all of us, and, especially after the act was passed, there was the crass utilitarian interest of the chemical manufacturers.

Before you shrug your shoulders and say, "Aha, that's the answer; why drag in all this philosophic stuff," I must mention that a sister act, the Federal Insecticide, Fungicide, and Rodenticide Act, has had quite a different fate. There are three differences: the insecticide act is much older; it is much more severe, since a half-million-dollar biological test is required for all

pesticides; and, most importantly, it deals only with
pesticides that even the manufacturers acknowledge are
dangerous poisons. Because of the latter, the pesticide
act includes none of the elaborate restrictions on EPA's
authority that complicate the toxic substances act, and
the pesticide manufacturers--including many of the very
same firms that have frustrated the toxic substances act
--have acquiesced almost cheerfully. But in the case of
the toxic substances act it is hard not to have reservations about requiring manufacturers to spend large sums to
gather information on the dangers of chemicals that almost
certainly are not dangerous. Such reasonable reservations
not only explain why the chemical manufacturers have re-
sisted but also explain why their resistance has been
tolerated and, thus far, successful. This confusion about
what we really want to do about new chemicals, a few of
which are possibly toxic, has led to half-hearted support
and to paralysis in implementaiton.

PROPOSED SOLUTIONS

There are many other examples of fundamental conflicts in these and in the other environmental protection
programs, but I'll rest my case with these three. They
illustrate the pervasive indecisiveness that places the
administrators in the predicament of having to strive for
two inconsistent goals at the same time. Generally speaking, neither goal is attained.

This moral predicament is not an easy one to get out
of, nor is it the only obstacle that stands between us and
the safe and pleasant environment we all desire. But it
would make progress easier if we could resolve it.

Most economists, but not I, are addicted to an easy
method for solving all such goal conflicts. It consists
of establishing a scale, nearly always money, for measur-
ing the importance of the different goals and then advo-
cating the decisions that make the sum of all these values
as great as possible. This is a sweeping version of utilitarianism that subsumes respect for human rights under
the broad umbrella of general welfare. It is a spurious
solution, however. The economists who advocate it are
deluding themselves, since they also believe in the sanctity of our fundamental rights and immunities.

There is, in fact, no way to place a monetary value
on a violation of somebody's rights. That does not mean
that societies and governments never violate individual
rights; on the contrary, they do so routinely. But each
violation is a serious matter and can be justified only by

advancing some goal of commanding social importance. So
this easy way out is only make-believe, one that cannot
be, and is not, used in practice.

The only clue to a solution that I know of is in the
work of American philosopher (naturally) John Rawls
(1971), who squarely confronted the inconsistency in the
ethical principles he had inherited. I suggest a revised
version of his solution, but he mustn't be blamed for my
revision.

Rawls's idea is to divide all social goals affected
by a decision into two classes, which I shall call primary
values and secondary values. The primary values are those
that concern the respect for natural rights; the secondary
values are those included in the general welfare in the
ordinary sense of the term. The effect of a decision on
the secondary values is measured most conveniently by the
benefit-cost calculus already discussed. But those are
only the secondary values. The primary values are primary
in importance and must be considered separately. They
concern losses, suffering, and even death inflicted on
people through no fault of their own.

Here is where I diverge from Rawls's own position.
He maintains that no diminution in the respect for primary
values can be justified by any increase in the attainment
of the secondary, utilitarian values--in effect, that no
one should legitimately be harmed, not even one angina patient, for example, no matter how great the resultant improvement in the general welfare. I believe that such an
extremely fastidious society could not survive. Although
such violations are not to be taken lightly, neither can
we hope to avoid them completely.

The situation we now confront is this. We must
choose between two decisions, such as two different levels
for the CO ambient standard, Decision A and Decision B.
Suppose Decision A contributes more to the general welfare
than does Decision B. That would be enough for a thor-
oughgoing utilitarian, but it is not enough for us. We
have to check to see whether Decision A invades any of the
basic human rights more than does Decision B. If not, all
is well and Decision A is the preferable alternative. But
if Decision A does violate some people's rights more seriously than does Decision B, we are likely to be confronted with what Calabresi (1978) has aptly called a tragic
choice.

Circumstances differ vastly, so there seems to be no
possibility of a formula analogous to the one that can be
applied to the secondary benefits for deciding whether the

violations are justified in any particular instance. But,
though he does not believe in making such choices, Rawls
has proposed a standard by which they can be made. Each
of us would have to ask himself or herself earnestly the
following hypothetical question: If I did not know how
the decision would apply to me, would I prefer to live in
a society that chose Decision A or one that chose Decision
B? Let us consider an example. The chances are about one
in ten thousand that I will suffer from angina pectoris.
Would I prefer to live in a society that permitted a pollution level that would accelerate my attacks (in order to
increase the general welfare, including my own, by $100
million a year) to living in one that would not?

That is not an easy question to answer, and it is not
the same as the standard economist's question, "If I were
an angina sufferer, how much would I be willing to pay to
have the onset of an attack deferred by half a minute?"
The answer to the economist's question, if it can be as-
certained, belongs in the ordinary account of benefits and
costs. The answer to the Rawlsian question relates to the
kind of ethical standards an individual would like a society to maintain, with special attention to its reluc-
tance to infringe on individual rights. I do not think
that our preferences in this regard can be described in
general terms, at least not until we have gained a great
deal of experience in answering the kinds of specific
questions that I have proposed. So such questions must be
posed again and again.

One more example will illustrate how hard, or how
easy, those questions can be. Suppose you did not know in
which country you were going to live after this year but
you did know that if the United States continues to use
synthetic chemicals, two toxic waste depositories will
have to be established in each state, regardless of the
wishes of the people living nearby. Would you prefer to
live in a country that permitted chemical production gen-
erating toxic wastes or in one that banned it?

One last matter. I propose this approach as a solution to the problem of releasing EPA, and other agencies
as well, from the contradictory mandates that they now receive. Could it really do so? Obviously, I think it
could. The agency would have to perform the ordinary benefit-cost analysis that it now is required to go through,
at the same time and using the same data keeping track of
the extent to which human rights are invaded under the
various options. Finally in most instances, it would have

to form a considered judgment as to whether a decent and humane society would consider the more advantageous economic choice to be advantageous enough to justify the accompanying infringements of individual rights.

I am sure this approach is possible in the kind of society that prefers such a procedure to the current one of espousing infeasible or contradictory goals.

REFERENCES

Calabresi, Guido. 1978. Tragic Choices. New York: Norton.
Friedman, Milton, 1982. Capitalism and Freedom. Chicago: University of Chicago Press.
Mill, John Stuart. 1963. Collected Works. Toronto: University of Toronto Press.
Nozick, Robert. 1981. Philosophical Explanations. Cambridge, Mass.: Harvard University Press, Belknap.
Rawls, John. 1971. A Theory of Justice. Cambridge: Harvard Univerity Press, Belknap.

6 *Economic Science and Economic Policy*

ARNOLD C. HARBERGER

INTRODUCTION

The role of representative of the neoclassical tradition of economic science I find easy to accept, for it fits well with my own conception of what my life and career in economics has been all about. I see economics as a science in the true sense of the word--a discipline in which theories are evolved that attempt to explain observable events, in which there is a constant confrontation between events and the predictions or implications of our theories, and in which our ways of viewing the world change through time as our theoretical framework improves and as we better learn how to distill and interpret the facts before us.

The science of economics has roots going back more than 200 years, and I for one have always been mindful of the great tradition of thinking and of observation that we have inherited. Economic science has evolved through time, and whenever there has been a so-called "revolution" in economic thought purporting to overturn a major part of the grand tradition, it has only been a matter of time before one of two things has happened: the "revolutionary" idea has turned out to be wrong or the "revolutionary" idea has turned out to be (less revolutionary than was initially thought) yet another step in the evolving corpus of economic thought. I write, then, out of a background of great respect for the appreciation of the science of economics as it has developed over decades and centuries.

Economic science has a great deal to say about economic policy, and I will review some of the more important policy insights that the study of economic science brings. But at this point, I want to emphasize three different

© Arnold C. Harberger; printed with permission of the author.

aspects. (1) Economic science can be useful in a great
many different kinds of political environments. (2) Economic goals are not the only goals; a certain amount of
trading off--giving up some economic benefits when this is
a necessary price for obtaining political, social, or
other benefits--is perfectly healthy. (3) Sometimes, too,
policymakers find they are forced to accept inferior economic solutions, not because they are trading off to obtain some other benefit that they recognize as a genuine
desideratum but because they feel forced by political
realities to adopt a position that they consider to be
only third or fourth or fifth or tenth best, or even
worse.

   This latter point is very important, because in most
intellectual discussions of economic policy it is virtually taken for granted that noneconomic considerations, when
they become relevant, are "good." One must realize that,
along with "good" noneconomic objectives that reflect al-
truistic and humanistic motivations and that seek greater
degrees of liberty and human dignity for citizens, there
are also noneconomic decisions that reflect the paying off
of political debts, the yielding to the pressure of special interest groups, or the working of even more repre-
hensible motivations.

   The conclusion, when thinking along these lines, is
that while noneconomic considerations are certainly important in many instances, and perhaps painfully necessary
in others, they are not, in principle, part of the discipline of economics. Their nature varies greatly from time
to time and from place to place. And, more important,
economists as such have no particular reason to be more
expert than others at handling these noneconomic considerations. In general, economists will have to be a party to
any decision-making process in which economic and noneconomic considerations are weighed one against the other.
But the natural role for economists in this process is to
present in an adequate fashion the economic considerations, the economic costs and benefits of one alternative
policy package versus another, and so forth. One can pre-
pare for this role by taking good university economics
courses and/or by carefully studying the best recent professional literature in economics. On the other hand, it
is not at all easy to design a course or write a treatise
that will teach economists a systematic framework for
dealing with noneconomic matters in a policy context. It
is important to appreciate what development economics was

like, as a body of thought, in the 1950s and the advances
in economic thinking and the events that have changed the
focus of development economics thinking since then.

DEVELOPMENT ECONOMICS IN THE 1950s AND EARLY 1960s
        To characterize the beginning of this period, the de-
gree to which the thinking of the time placed physical
capital investment at the center of the stage must be emphasized. In the Harrod-Domar model of economic growth
(Harrod 1939, 1948, 1952, 1963, 1974; Domar 1946, 1947,
1957), output grew only because of increases in the
capital stock. Its key equation was

$$\Delta Y = \mu \ \Delta K \tag{6.1}$$

where Y is output (GDP) and K is the nation's physical
capital stock. This equation assumes all of the growth of
output stems from physical capital investment. If, following the common practice of that time, one takes as the
best estimate of the parameter μ the existing capital-output ratio K/Y, one sees that not only are increments of
output solely explained by increments of capital, but the
total of output is fully explained by the total stock of
capital:

$$Y = \mu K \tag{6.2}$$

        This, of course, left little scope (really none at
all) for other factors and forces in the growth process.
And there can be no doubt that this extreme vision of the
world would not have gained the widespread acceptance that
it did were it not for another strand in the intellectual
mainstream of the time, namely, the notion that the less
developed economies were suffering from surplus labor.
Labor was thought to be in surplus not in the sense that
there was a lot of it working with relatively little capital, resulting in relatively low marginal productivity
and consequently low wages, but rather in the much stricter sense that its marginal productivity was zero. Capital
investment was critical not just for its own sake, as it
were, but because it gave employment to labor that would
otherwise be unemployed and because the labor was paid not
out of its own marginal product but out of the marginal
product of capital.
        Out of this conceptual framework grew in the late
1950s and early 1960s a whole literature of sophisticated

mathematical planning models. These models joined the
concept of fixed capital-output ratios to the concept of
the input-output matrix. Labor might be in surplus, but
material inputs were not, if only because scarce capital
was required for their production. The new class of models were thus built on two sets of rigidities. One was
the fixity of the capital-output ratio itself in each separate activity of the economy:

$$X_i = \mu_i K_i \tag{6.3}$$

where X_i is the output of activity i and K_i is the capital
employed in its production. The other was the fixed link
between the output of any good and its required inputs of
other kinds:

$$X_{ij} = a_{ij} X_j, \qquad X_i = \sum_j X_{ij} + X_{if} \tag{6.4}$$

where X_{ij} is the amount of X_i used in the production of
X_j, A_{ij} is the input-output coefficient linking the one to
the other, and X_{if} is the amount of X_i used to satisfy the
final demand of the economy--consumption plus direct investment.

These principles were the basis of elaborate planning
models, using which planners were supposed to set targets
of final demand and in which the economy was supposed to
be organized so as to produce the amount of each input
needed to feed, directly and indirectly, the production of
the targeted package of outputs. Targets were to be
checked in advance to see if they were unfeasible, that
is, if they required more scarce resources (principally
capital) than would likely be made available (through national savings and foreign aid) in the planned period. If
they turned out to be unfeasible they were scaled down until they were within the feasible set.

This type of approach to the planning process probably reached its apogee in India in the late 1950s and the
1960s. Targets were preplanned for hundreds of separate
industries and activities, and a whole panoply of state
controls (such as imports licenses, investment licenses,
credit allocations, and materials quotas) were used in an
attempt to make the economy conform to the plan. Such was
the naivete of many in the economics profession in the
period around 1960 that a substantial group of development
economists at that time regarded Indian planning as a model of "how it should be done."

INTELLECTUAL FOUNDATIONS OF THE CURRENT
VIEW OF THE DEVELOPMENT PROCESS
    Before attempting to sketch some of the elements that
helped bring the profession to what I believe is the current view of the development process, let me emphasize
that the picture I have sketched of development economics
in the 1950s and early 1960s does not cover every development economist. There were some--notably Simon Kuznets
(1966) and T. W. Schultz (1964) among the leaders of the
profession and also notably the cadre of World Bank professionals who were fighting the battles of economic development in daily combat--who always appreciated the full
complexity of the process and never succumbed to the naive
oversimplification that characterized the development literature of the time. In many respects these people can
be said to have held already in the 1950s a vision of the
development process very similar to the one toward which
the profession as a whole has moved over the past few decades.
    The fact is that while some individuals learn very
fast or see the truth from the very beginning the profession as a whole learns slowly, possibly without any prominent individuals changing their minds (rather, as new
generations of professional leaders succeed their prede-
cessors). At least four major developments in economic
theory contributed to the changes that took place in the
profession's view of the development process: (1) the
modern theory of economic growth, (2) the theory of effective protection, (3) revisionism in macroeconomic theory,
and (4) the professionalization of policy economics.

The Modern Approach to Economic Growth
    I was tempted to label this discussion "the modern
theory of economic growth," but discretion and (I hope)
good judgment prevailed. The use of the term approach
rather than theory is dictated by the fact that what is
involved is the application of solid, time-tested, old
theoretical propositions to the careful analysis of the
growth process. This is what was done by writers like
Solow (1956, 1957, 1962, 1970), Kendrick (1961, 1976),
Denison (1962, 1967, 1969), and Abramovitz (1956, 1959),
who thereby helped bring about a major change in the way
the economic profession as a whole looked at the process
of development. To summarize the nature of the change,
one can say that the key feature consisted of shaking
loose the tight link that the earlier view had established between capital and output, along with the corollary that capital investment was the sole source of

economic growth. In a macroeconomic version, the new
approach decomposed the growth rate as follows:

$$\frac{\Delta Y}{Y} = s_L \frac{\Delta L}{L} + s_K \frac{\Delta K}{K} + R \tag{6.5}$$

where L is the employed labor force, K is the capital
stock, and Y is output. The shares of labor and capital
in aggregate output are s_L and s_K. The equation decom-
poses the growth rate of output into a part, $s_L(\Delta L/L)$, attributed to the growth of the employed labor force, another part, $s_K(\Delta K/K)$, attributed to the growth of the capital
stock, and finally a residual, R, representing the net effect of other forces. The basis of attributing these particular contributions to labor and capital was straightforward neoclassical theory: each factor was presumed to
have a marginal product equal to its earnings. The great
discovery that set the profession to thinking came from
the empirical finding that labor and capital together only
account for a fraction (often less than half) of observed
growth. The residual was important in almost every case
and was the dominant source of major differences in growth
rates over time and across countries.
     The residual was initially thought of as a coeffi-
cient of technical advance (since it effectively measured
the growth in output per unit of input), but it was quick-
ly recognized to be a composite of the effects of many
different forces, including the following:

     1. Improvement in the quality of labor through edu-
cation, experience and on-the-job training
     2. Reallocation of resources from low-productivity
to higher productivity uses, either through normal market
forces or through the reduction of barriers or distortions
     3. Exploitation of economies of scale
     4. Improved ways of combining resources to produce
goods and services, not just at the level of new machines
or processes but also by relatively mundane adjustments at
the level of the factory or the farm

     The recognition of the importance of all these fac-
tors enriched the profession's vision of the growth process and brought it much closer to reality in its policy
prescriptions and judgments.

The Theory of Effective Protection
     One of the most profound and important recent

advances in economics is the theory of effective protection and the wealth of empirical studies of this phenomenon. The concept of effective protection is quite simple. A Mexican tariff of 30 percent on shirts indeed provides 30 percent protection if all the materials and resources used in making the shirt are Mexican. But if some of them are imported the story is quite different. For example, if woolen cloth is imported at zero duty and accounts for half the value of the shirt at international prices, the thirty points of protection are concentrated only on the Mexican value added, giving it effective protection of 60 percent. And if cashmere cloth is imported, accounting for 90 percent of the value of the shirt at international prices, the effective protection of Mexican value added turns out to be 300 percent.

These examples show how effective protection can turn out to be very different from the nominal rate of tariff. Empirical studies (notably those by Bela Balassa [1970], Jagdish Bhagwati [1964], and Anne Krueger [1974]) have shown how high, typically, are the effective rates of protection and how heavy are the burdens, in terms of resulting economic inefficiency, that many developing countries have (as it were) imposed on themselves. These studies have provided the evidence of why trade liberalization is in most cases a high-priority, high-payoff component of a program for economic development. Simultaneously, effective protection theory has given a strong message with respect to the design of economic policy. In brief that message is that unless there is a uniform tariff on all imported products--capital goods and materials inputs as well as final products, and goods that cannot be produced domestically as well as those that can--one cannot even know with a reasonable degree of certainty what the effective protection of a product is. The 30 percent Mexican tariff on men's shirts in the example makes a 60 percent effective protection of the activity of converting imported woolen cloth into men's shirts and a 300 percent effective protection of the conversion of imported cashmere cloth. But even these protection rates are ephemeral; they will change with every movement of the world price of wool and cashmere. All the confusion about what the rate of effective protection is can be avoided only by having a uniform and general tariff on all imports. So while the first lesson emerging from effective protection theory and analysis is to liberalize tariffs, the second, to the

extent that liberalization is incomplete, is to equalize
the tariff schedule.

Revisionism in Macroeconomic Theory

There was a time in the 1950s and early 1960s when
macroeconomists taught and wrote about fine-tuning the
economy to achieve any desired goal, and even about "out-
lawing the business cycle." One no longer hears such talk
today. Part of the change is due to a decade of stagfla-
tion and recession. Probably more important has been the
impact of recent advances in macroeconomic theory, which
have given the economics profession a much humbler yet (I
believe) much more realistic vision of its role and task.
We cannot fine-tune the economy, says the new macroeconomics, nor can we outlaw the business cycle. The best we
can do is create a climate that obviates unnecessary confusion, misperception, and mistakes by economic agents
throughout the economy, to adopt a good policy rule, let
people know what it is, and stick to it. This is what the
new macroeconomics teaches us. It is certainly a far cry
from the utopian planning of the future of an economy,
sector by sector and product by product, described earlier
in the chapter.

The Professionalization of Policy Economics

This is a difficult subject for me to treat, perhaps
because my own experience has been too close to the
events. The best introduction may be to note a thought
that occurred to me at a meeting of public finance economists sponsored by the National Bureau of Economic Research (NBER) a few years ago: nearly everything about
the conference would have been different had it been held
fifteen or twenty years earlier. People then were concerned with the effects of taxation on labor effort and on
saving. They took seriously the so-called welfare costs
of taxation. When dealing with the issue of general,
broad-based taxes, they took seriously the alternative of
a progressive consumption expenditure tax. When considering almost any problem, they set it out in such a way that
it yielded a result that was in one sense or another an
optimum.

The development economics of the 1950s and prerevi-
sionist macroeconomics both contained more than a little
flavor of the "free lunch" or "easy way out" solutions to
problems. For example, the balanced budget multiplier of

elementary textbook fame asserted that the government providing school lunches that parents had previously paid for and then taxing the parents in an amount equal to the cost of the lunches would somehow miraculously produce an increase in national product, income, and welfare. Another example comes from the "two-gap" literature, one of the recent, more sophisticated manifestations of the programming approach discussed at the end of the section on development economics in the 1950s. I have heard it seriously contended that $1 million of additional foreign aid would add $10 million to the product of a country. (My response to this is that under those circumstances it would be easy for the aid-giving agency to extract from the country in question the equivalent of, say, $2 or $3 million in counterpart funds!)

No such conjurer's tricks were put forward by the young policy economists at the NBER conference. They were ready to assign a proper cost to every resource and a proper value to human effort. The economics they applied was the battery of tools and concepts that had emerged from the two-hundred year history of the profession. With this conceptual framework they were able to provide answers to many questions, broad as well as narrow and extending in scope from the national economy down to the economy of individual households. Their answers entailed no free lunches, no miracles. But they were professional solutions to difficult problems, solutions that, if adopted, would improve the functioning of the economy in question.

The connection between all this and our profession's view of the process of economic development is that the same sort of attitude that was reflected in the public finance conference has carried over into discussions of economic policy in developing countries. The more professional approach to policy questions in general must also be taken when addressing the policy problems of developing countries.

SOME MODEST LESSONS OF EXPERIENCE

Economists have learned a few lessons from observing the behavior of a whole host of developing countries over the last twenty-five or thirty years. This list, not intended to be exhaustive, deals with things that we have learned about the usefulness of various economic techniques on the one hand and with more specific policy lessons on the other. I believe that most veterans of institutions like the International Monetary Fund, the World

Bank, and the various regional development banks would basically agree with these inferences.

Big Macroeconomic Models Have Not Helped Significantly
The most extensive experiments with big macroeconomic models have probably taken place in the United States. Specific ones that come to mind are the so-called Brookings Model, the FRB-MIT model, and the Wharton-EFU model. These models have played a minor role in the area of forecasting; what they have not done is give any significant help or insight into general policy formation. Even huge models are, in a sense, too crude to help design a given tax (such as a value-added tax or an income tax), let alone an entire tax system. So it is in other areas; even the biggest models are too crude to serve as guides as to whether to accept a particular investment project.

Input-Output Models Have Not Helped Either
Early in life I was lucky to learn the truth about input-output tables. It was in the year 1951, and I was working for President Truman's Materials Policy Commission. My task was to develop projections for U.S. and world demand for each of a great many minerals and fuels. As a staff member of the commission I was given access to a supersecret, 500-by-500 input-output matrix, which was in the custody of the Defense Department. Imagine my dismay on finding that such a matrix did not discriminate between copper, lead, zinc, and tin. There were pig iron, steel, coal, aluminum, and "other nonferrous metals." Obviously I had to turn elsewhere to find a basis for projections for copper, lead, zinc, and tin--not to mention antimony, sulfur, manganese, and magnesium.

The general lesson that we have learned about input-output tables is that their coefficients have no relevant implications for policy. If on the average the rubber products industry uses 5 cents worth of nonferrous metals per dollar of its own output, what help is that fact to a policymaker? It certainly does not mean that every time capacity in the rubber industry increases, capacity in the nonferrous metals industry will have to increase, too. It may, in fact, be that most nonferrous metals are not used at all in the rubber industry. Perhaps the coefficient is the result of a statistical quirk, like a rubber company producing rubber-covered copper wire. That might be the only place in the rubber industry where any nonferrous metal is used at all. These and similar examples, and in particular actually trying to work with specific industry output "predictions" or "requirements" derived from input-output tables, is what has led to disillusionment on the part of veteran observers of and participants in the policy process in developing countries.

Industries and Sectors Are Not Usually Good Objects of Policy

The textile industry makes everything from children's shoes to tents, from sheets to cashmere sweaters. What policy problem would lead a government to want to treat the production of these things differently from the production of nontextiles? The same question applies to the rubber and rubber products industry; to stone, clay, and glass products; and to chemicals. The principal exceptions to this rule occur in cases (such as airlines and pharmaceuticals) in which the industry category pretty well defines the firms that are the object of a legitimate regulatory purpose (safety and possibly fares in the case of airlines and purity and "dangerous substance control" in the case of pharmaceuticals).

Basically what is at issue is fitting the right policy to the right target. As in the Mexican shirt industry, where a wage subsidy would be far preferable to a tariff as an incentive to create employment in a particular activity, it usually turns out that the proper objects of most sensible policies are better delineated by criteria other than industry. In several countries there is legislation to help small businesses and yet further legislation to help small businesses owned by members of racial and other minorities. There is legislation to help poor families with dependent children and to help with the medical care of people who are poor and/or over sixty-five. There is legislation to regulate the excessive production of smoke from factories and the emission of contaminants into rivers and streams. This type of legislation at least withstands initial examination. Most laws delineating an industry as the object do not survive even the simplest test of whether the affected entities really belong together as a single class, as objects of a particular policy.

Projections Are Useful Adjuncts to Public Sector Planning and Budgeting but Not Central to the Process

I am not only the author of one of the first sets of long-term projections of the U.S. economy but also a veteran of many projection exercises in planning offices, central banks, ministries of finance, and project

evaluations in various parts of the world (including
Panama, Honduras, Costa Rica, and Chile). The truth is
that most important policy decisions are fundamentally independent of specific quantitative projections. A value-
added tax is always better than a cascade-type tax. A
strong move to equalize tariff rates in a system that previously had very disparate rates is overwhelmingly likely
to be a good move, again regardless of the result of the
projections. To get rid of policies that are obviously
bad, to get rid of the skeletons in the economic policy
closet, should be the first task of planners and policymakers. The second task perhaps should be to try to bring
some coherency to the patchwork quilt of policies inherited from the past. This is not an easy task. Interest
groups and pressure groups are always present, and one or
more of these groups is likely to organize resistance to
any legislation resulting in change. Policymakers cannot
take refuge in simple projections as an excuse for not
pursuing the general public interest in modifying and improving existing laws.

Contingency Planning

A corollary to the comparative unimportance of projections is the importance of contingency planning. Time
spent in building big models, creating input-output tables, and making beautifully detailed and consistent projections of what the economy will (or might possibly) look
like ten years hence would be better spent in contingency
planning for potential disasters. The world has survived
two major oil price rises in the 1970s; some countries
managed adaptation to the crisis better than others. On
the whole, those who survived the oil crises better were
those who thought in advance about the possibility of such
an event. Secondly, those who survived better were those
who recognized that what was involved was a genuine, ex-
ternally imposed reduction in real income. This recognition, too, was an aspect of good economic policy. To di-
agnose a situation correctly is often 90 percent of the
battle. Those who lost most as a consequence of the oil
crises were those who did not plan in advance for the contingency and, when it came, did not recognize it as a reduction in real income that no currency policy decision
could reverse.

Marginal Tax Rates of Over 50 Percent Do Not Make Sense

Our learning process in these situations took place
more in developed than in less developed countries. I can

remember the time when the top marginal income tax rate in
the United States was 91 percent and when the corresponding rate in the United Kingdom was 95 percent. We learned
by painful experience that these high rates yielded little
total revenue and provided great incentive to people to
spend time, energy, and money discovering ways to shelter
their incomes. Today the public finance fraternity is
pretty much in agreement that rates higher than 50 percent
are counterproductive and should be avoided.

Severe Limits to Using Taxation to Improve
Income Distribution in Developing Countries

The lesson is very clear; even in countries like the
United States, the United Kingdom, and the Netherlands,
the distribution of after-tax income is not greatly different from the distribution of before-tax income. The
Gini-coefficient may change from .38 to .35 but not much
more. To achieve an equivalent effect, a developing country would have to adopt somewhat similar tax policies.
But, for practical purposes, that is impossible. In the
United States for the last several decades a 50 percent
marginal tax rate was reached at between 5 and 6 times the
then per capita GDP. In what Latin American country of
$1000-per-capita income can one plausibly imagine marginal
tax rates of 50 percent taking effect for all income over
$5000? The same is true for the more advanced countries,
with incomes ranging around $2000 per capita. Who can
imagine, let alone propose, a marginal tax rate of 50 percent taking effect for all income even over $10,000?

Since one cannot seriously contemplate these possibilities, one must accept that the tax systems of developing countries will exhibit a smaller difference between
the pretax and posttax distributions of income than in
countries like the United States and the United Kingdom.
This means that the tax system will not greatly alter the
underlying distribution of income.

Basic Needs Are More Important than Income Distribution

Perhaps the easiest way to demonstrate this proposition is to consider the negative income tax. Low incomes
accrue to many people. On the whole, adolescents and re-
tired people on pensions account for perhaps half or more
of the low incomes in a community; these cases do not reflect serious financial distress or unmet basic needs. A
truly needy family with zero income could be cared for at
a minimum standard with a subsidy (negative income tax)

equal to, say, 2/3 of one per capita GDP. But the income
tax schedule has to turn positive at some point. If that
point happens to be 2/3 of one per capita GDP, then the
marginal tax rate between zero income and this particular
point would work out to be 100 percent. If the point at
which positive income tax starts to be paid is one per
capita GDP, the marginal tax rate between zero income and
that point would be 66 2/3 percent. This type of marginal tax rate has devastating implications for the incentive to work of adolescents and others. Moreover, no society could afford to pay all its zero income people an
amount equal to 2/3 of one per capita GDP. Those with unmet basic needs, must be distinguished from the rest who
basically are able to cope with the situation.

     We do not want to subsidize middle-class teenagers or
retirees on annuities or wealthy businessmen who for one
or two years find themselves with negative or zero incomes. We do want to provide for basic needs that would
otherwise go unmet. We need criteria that are as clear as
possible to distinguish basic need from nonbasic need situations. Spending public funds to meet nonbasic needs is
a waste of money and often grossly unfair to boot. Even
rich countries are finding they can't afford such expenditures; poor ones can afford them even less. The final
lesson is this. The meeting of basic human needs is a
profoundly moral (as well as an intelligent political)
goal for governments; the provision of free public services, direct or hidden subsidies, and other benefits to
citizens who are not in the basic need category can be
both demoralizing and dangerous. The precedents a government sets, particularly in budgetary terms, call into
question the criteria of equity on which it is operating
(if one undeserving group can feed at the public trough,
why not another, and yet another?)

"Political Prices" Are the Great Peril
of Public Enterprises

     I am proud to say that I have never taken a dogmatic
position on the issue of public enterprises. Probably
this stems from the fact that I early became involved in
the operations of several of them. In Latin America, for
example, I have worked directly with half a dozen electricity enterprises (CFE in Mexico, INE in Honduras, ICE
in Costa Rica, ELECTROBRAS in Brazil, and ENDESA and
Chilectra in Chile). Through these contacts I have gained
great respect for the professional quality of their

personnel, their dedication to their tasks, and, on the
whole, their overall operations. Public sector enterprises have distinguished themselves outside the electricity field, as well. For example, at the present time
Renault may be one of the most efficient and best managed
automobile companies in the world.

Thus there is no question that public enterprises can
be efficient and successful if given the right environment, the right incentives, the right motivation. At the
same time, public enterprises run far greater risks than
private ones, owing, in general, to their political ex-
posure. They find it difficult to cut out unprofitable
operations or to reduce staff when that is what is called
for, find themselves pressed to pay their lower skilled
workers significantly more than the market wage, and often
find themselves limited in what they can pay their top ex-
ecutives. On the side of selling products, they find it
much more difficult than do private sector enterprises to
raise their prices to reflect cost increases and they often are required by government policy to provide services
at a sizable loss.

All these situations reflect what I call "political
prices." Political prices are the bane of public enterprises. If they can be avoided or eliminated, the enterprise stands a reasonable chance of success. If political
prices are the rule, there is no hope for the success of
the enterprise.

Realism forces me to recognize that there are circumstances where government policy should insist that some
goods or services be provided at less than cost (rural
electrification is an excellent case in point). In such
cases the best rule to follow is for the government to
give the public enterprise a direct subsidy from the public sector budget to cover the implicit loss involved and
permit the enterprise to operate as a business, covering
costs and earning a reasonably competitive rate of return.

No Historical Justification of Prices

Many of the worst instances of prices totally unre-
flective of economic reality have come from attempts to
maintain some preexisting price in the face of changing
circumstances. Rent controls in New York and other U.S.
cities are a good example, and there are many more. During the 1970s there were two episodes in which the world
market price of sugar reached 50 cents per pound, or more.
Some countries refused to recognize this reality and

maintained their internal price at the historical level of around 10 cents. My colleague Professor D. Gale Johnson has estimated that such a policy reduced Brazil's net foreign exchange position by a sum approaching $1 billion in the two episodes.

The temptation to stick with historical pricing is obviously strong, but it is one that good makers of economic policy will resist. The lesson of economics is very simple: prices should always function to reflect relative scarcity, and over the middle and longer run economic forces should operate to make them reflect the relative resource cost of producing different goods and services.

COMPARING SUCCESSES AND FAILURES

I vividly recall the economic development discussions of the mid-1950s, perhaps because I was myself so new to the field. Among many other things, I remember ridiculing assertions that inflation, protectionism, dirigismo, or whatever, played a decisive role in impeding the development of a nation's economy. I guess I still would stand by those judgments, but certainly from a very different perspective than I had at the time. Then my perception was that we simply did not have evidence on which to distinguish winners from losers in the struggle for economic development. Now I feel that we have ample, perhaps overwhelming evidence but that, in such an exceedingly multifaceted and complex process with many decisions, no single mistake is vital.

The difference between then and now is that we have clear-cut cases of success and failure and we can discern certain characteristic differences between. The success stories include Malaysia, Singapore, Hong Kong, Korea, Taiwan, Greece, Spain, Brazil from the mid-1960s, Mexico from the mid-1950s into the 1970s, and Panama throughout the 1960s and into the 1970s. The failures include cases of dramatic collapse, such as occurred in Brazil in 1964, Indonesia in 1966, Chile in 1973, and Argentina in 1976, and of chronic stagnation, such as Uruguay, which had a negative rate of growth of per capita income between 1950 and 1973. Jamaica and Ghana also had negative rates of real growth in the latter half of the 1970s.

I perceive that the successful countries approached economic policy decisions with a different attitude than did the disaster cases. The successful countries were much more likely to see policy decisions as technical

problems of "doing the right thing," while the unsuccessful countries were more likely to see them as political
problems. Moreover (especially since the political
process pervades all governmental decisions), the unsuccessful cases were characterized by governments that pro-
mised more than they could deliver, that had romantic
dreams about what should be done and an unrealistic disregard of the constraints and costs of doing it. The
crises of the unsuccessful countries generally came at the
end of a period of expansion of government activity with a
heavily populist flavor, giving the people things that
pleased them politically but doing so while ignoring, or
at least failing to provide adequately for, the costs.

The successful countries, by contrast, tended to view
their policy problems as technical ones, in which costs
should not be ignored. That simple statement has implications for electricity pricing as well as for project ap-
praisal, for food and housing subsidies as well as for in-
fant-industry protection. While the successful countries
all have skeletons in their economic policy closets, they
have far fewer than the unsuccessul ones. Their technical
or professional batting average on policy decisions is
much higher, and that, I suspect, is why they won.

It should be clear by now that this point of view ex-
plicitly recognizes the complexity of the growth process
and rather truculently refuses to single out any specific
factor or source of growth as predominant. Yet there are
at least two areas of policy that in some sense cover many
layers of detailed decisions; one is the issue of the degree of openness of the economy, the other the extent to
which a country resorts to the inflation tax.

Consider first the issue of openness. Whereas in the
decade of the 1960s the typical middle-income country had
an export growth rate of 5.4 percent per year, the median
rate for the ten successful countries was 10.5 percent.
In the period 1970-1977 the corresponding figures were 5.1
percent for the typical middle-income country and 9.8 percent for the successful ones (World Bank 1979, 140-41).
Export expansion was a critical part of the process of
growth in the successful countries, and I am willing to
risk my professional reputation to assert that their export growth in these periods did not come as if by an act
of God, from the outside, with these countries simply ben-
efitting from their luck. On the contrary, a multiplicity
of policy choices aimed at closer linkage with the world
economy underlay the growth of exports. Perhaps I can
convey an inkling of what is at stake here by pointing out

that in 1980 India's exports were $14.3 billion, while
Taiwan's were $10 billion, Korea's $22.3 billion, Brazil's
$25 billion, Hong Kong's $22.4 billion, Singapore's $24
billion, and Spain's $34.1 billion. And of these export-
ers at least four (Taiwan, Hong Kong, Korea, and Spain)
had experienced increases in the dollar value of their exports between 1960 and 1980, greater than India's total
1980 exports. The policies that contribute to a closed
economy (well represented by India) tend invariably to in-
hibit exports, while those that contribute to an open economy tend to expand exports. An open economy will tend to
have high exports and imports, relative to its GNP or
other aggregate measure, a closed economy low exports and
imports relative to the same measures. The successful
countries, without exception, opted in the periods of
their greatest growth for the open economy.

On the inflation front, it is fair to say that the
successful countries exhibited prudent behavior. Their
median rate of inflation in the 1960s was 3.3 percent,
while that of the industrialized countries was 4.2 percent. In 1970-1977 their median inflation rate was 12.2
percent, while for the industrial countries it was 9.4
percent. Among them only Brazil is an outlier in the
inflation dimension, and Brazil also has the distinction
of being included among the unsuccessful cases. The periods of crisis of the unsuccessful cases were characterized by extreme inflation, and even in their less-bad
years they have characteristically resorted regularly to
the inflation tax. Including Brazil, the median annual
inflation rate of the countries listed as crisis countries
was 46 percent in the 1960s and 68 percent in 1970-1977
(World Bank 1979, 126-27). These figures do not represent
the most dramatic inflationary experience of any of these
countries, which tended to be coincident with the break-
down of the economic system and at its worst typically
ranged from 100 to 400 percent per year.

A MODERN VIEW OF THE DEVELOPMENT PROCESS
On the theory side, many of the blinders that inhib-
ited clear vision have been removed as a consequence of
intellectual advances on the one hand and of the concrete
experience of nations on the other. The essence of neoclassical economics is that productive factors tend to get
paid, at most, their marginal product, viewed from the
standpoint of the enterprise that pays them. We also know
that the social marginal product of a factor can be different from that seen by the enterprise. When a

divergence exists between private and social marginal products, economists identify it as a distortion. Distortions
can be of many types, but by far the most important among
them is taxes. Taxes quite obviously introduce a wedge
between the value that the end result of a productive service has to its users and the compensation that is effectively received (and perceived as true compensation) by
the person who provided that service. Other sources of
distortion include (1) monopoly and oligopoly profits,
which are really privately imposed and privately collected
taxes; (2) economies of scale, which generate marginal
productivity in excess of average productivity and, typically, in excess of factor remunerations (that is, activities with economies of scale should typically be subsid-
ized to correct for the distortion); (3) congestion in all
its forms, including what Anne Krueger (1974) has called
rent-seeking activity of all types (here the marginal social product of a resource or of an activity is less than
its private marginal product, and the activity should typically be taxed, or a common-property resource properly
priced, to correct for the distortion); (4) pollution,
contamination, and their opposites, which generate external benefits to particular activities.

  Consider, then, that all of these items that create
differences between the marginal social product and the
marginal private product of a resource in a given activity
are summarized in a measure, D_i, of the distortion applying there. Then let us express the growth of output by
the equation

$$\Delta Y = \sum_i \Delta L_i (w_i + D_i) + \sum_j \Delta K_j (r_j + D_j) + R \qquad (6.6)$$

  In this framework we must think of labor and capital
as classified into quite narrowly defined boxes. A
thirty-year-old engineer is more productive than a thirty-
year-old sweeper, so the labor force must be broken down
by occupation. Education also plays a role, as those with
more education tend to be more productive. Location can
be relevant, too, for the wages of workers of given type,
age, education, etc., need not be the same in different
regions. (In the United States there are significant differences between, say, Alaska and Mississippi; in India,
the differences, particularly in agricultural wages, between, say, the Punjab and Bihar, are vast.) Industry is
important as a characteristic of classification to the extent that distortions such as product taxes, product

monopoly elements, factor monopoly elements (union wages
in excess of the norm for equivalent workers), economies
of scale, and other distortions referred to above will
vary from industry to industry. But in principle if even
within an industry these distortions were to vary from
factory to factory, then the criterion of classification
ought to be narrowed down to the level of the factory.

Of course we never really do these things, but this
is nonetheless the way to think clearly, in modern terms,
about the process of economic growth. In principle, the
first term of equation (6.6) takes into account the contribution to the growth of, say, GNP from the following
sources, among others:

    1. the employment of labor previously unemployed

    2. the movement of labor from an activity with low
wages to an activity with high wages

    3. the movement of labor from an untaxed to a taxed
activity (GNP grows and the government gains tax revenues)

    4. the increase in the labor force of an activity
with economies of scale

    5. the improvement that occurs when a worker's
productivity is upgraded, be it through education,
experience, or on-the-job training

    6. the improvement that occurs when, by reducing
distortions, the government causes the use of labor to
increase in activities with positive distortions.

With respect to capital, the relevant categories are
different from those applying to labor. In general, the
principal criteria relate to the tax status of the capital
involved. This varies depending on whether financing is
in the form of equity (to the income to which the corporation income tax usually applies) or from debt (to which it
is not). It also varies depending on the nature of the
asset; some assets are subject to property or real estate
taxes, and others are not. Of course, when excise taxes
are involved they create distortions between the private
and the social marginal productivity of capital; hence
whenever they are present the classification of capital,
K_j should include the criterion of the industry in which
it is employed or the product it helps to produce.

The second term of equation (6.6) thus captures the
contribution to economic growth stemming from

    7. new investible funds that are injected into the
capital stock

   8. the negative growth stemming from the
depreciation or retirement of old components of the
capital stock
   9. the reallocation of capital between
low-productivity and high-productivity uses
   10. the movement of capital into activities with
positive distortions (taxes, monopoly profits, economies
of scale, or other positive externalities)

   The message of all this is that a simple and quite
straightforward approach, fully rooted in neoclassical
economic theory yet thoroughly capable of taking into account all sorts of distortions and market imperfections,
ends up explaining most of what in the earlier modern
macroeconomic analysis of growth, as represented by equation (6.5), would be stuck in the residual R. The residual in equation (6.6) would have to be much, much smaller
than that in equation (6.5) and could much more truly be
identified as a pure "technical advance."
   In short, the current version of modern growth analysis, as represented in equation (6.6) embodies quintes-
sential common sense. It is so simple that it hardly mer-
its the term theory, yet it is a theory, and a very powerful one in the sense that it helps to interpret events and
to make choices in many circumstances that arise as part
of daily experience in the real world. Above all it shows
that the incredible complexity of the growth process is
perfectly reasonable, perfectly plausible, perfectly consonant with common sense. Growth comes from using more
resources, on the one hand, and from using given resources
better, on the other. Within the latter category we have
the reduction of resource misallocations as well as the
improvement of the quality or productivity of human
agents.
   As a somewhat veteran exponent of this view of economic growth, I feel it is nothing more than where one
should arrive with common sense plus a modicum of intell-
igence. It should not be beyond the reach, for example,
of people in other disciplines. They may not be able to
do the detailed work involved in the analysis of programs,
policies, or projects, but they should be able to see the
basic sense of the analytical structure that is being applied.

POLICY: THE BATTLE IS FOUGHT IN THE TRENCHES
   The bottom line is that development economics, as it
is asked to confront the specific problems of developing

countries, in one way or another is virtually coincident
with applied welfare economics. Applied welfare economics
tells us many, many things. It tells us that inefficient
markets reduce the level of real income of an economy. It
tells us that some taxes are a lot worse, economically,
than others that strike by and large the same groups. It
tells us that protectionism inflicts its costs principally
on the societies that adopt it. It tells us that the inflation tax is typically a pretty bad tax, though policies
can be found to enable an economy to live with inflation
at a lower cost than many would surmise. It tells us that
many investment projects, particularly public investment
projects with political appeal, accumulate public funds
and resources and never provide a corresponding benefit.

Once the complexity of the process of growth is fully
recognized, the general lines of desirable policy become
quite clear, leading private decision makers in the direction of socially desirable actions. This means trying to
make private benefits and costs as close as possible to
social benefits and costs, that is to say, eliminating
government-produced distortions where possible and using
government policy to offset private distortions (such as
pollution and congestion) as well. Anyone who learns applied welfare economics need have no hesitancy in being
considered a development economist.

Each of the big issues highlighted earlier in this
chapter--protectionism and inflation--are captured and
dealt with under the rubric of applied welfare economics.
So too are the subtler problems associated with domestic
taxes and subsidies, with ceilings and floors for prices
or wages or interest rates. And finally there is the
level of investment projects, the real battle in the trenches. In any country the number of bad projects institut-
ed to inspire political enthusiasts and political support
usually outweighs by a factor of, say, five or more the
number of projects that really should be undertaken. The
task of project evaluation within government is without a
doubt that of "shooting down" bad projects.

Bad projects always (or nearly always) have strong
advocates. So long as a net contribution of government
funds is involved, the benefit perceived by the beneficiaries is likely to be greater than the cost to them. An
example is an irrigation dam in a certain Arizona county.
The citizens of that county know that the dam will enhance
their welfare. Why? Because they are probably only
paying from 2 to 20 percent of the cost of the dam. The
remainder is being paid by the rest of the taxpayers.

The primary task of a project authority or of a planning agency charged with the responsibility for projects is thus shooting down the bad projects. Such an agency must always and predominantly represent the interests of the taxpayer (who is paying most of the cost) against the interests of beneficiaries paying only a fraction of the cost. Whenever the beneficiaries pay the whole freight, the project authority can relax; whenever they pay less, the project evaluation authorities should be suspicious and vigilant.

Getting rid of bad projects is probably the most straightforward advice a development economist can give a typical government of a developing country. Such advice has to be right, because every government in the world undertakes at least a few bad projects each year. But programs and policies usually have a broader sanction and/or a wider clientele than the typical investment project, and the political resistance to a change in policy is obviously stronger. So an important part of the score assigned to the economic policy of a particular government depends on the degree to which it gives weight, in the decision process, to considerations of cost, on the one hand, and of benefits in the middle and long run, on the other.

Thus the modern view of economic growth has a natural policy counterpart in the methodology of applied welfare economics and of social cost-benefit analysis. A substantial group of experienced observers of the development process reached this conclusion a long time ago. This is far from saying that temptation has disappeared from the world and governments will from now on always have the prudence, wisdom, courage, and restraint to do the right thing. In private lives people struggle to overcome human failings, to have the better side of their nature win out over the baser; in public policy, too, there is (and will always be) a similar struggle. Economic science, and in particular the tools of applied welfare economics and modern cost-benefit analysis, are great forces for good in this mighty struggle.

CONCLUDING REMARKS

It is not possible to draw all the lessons that can be derived from the science of economics that would help to inform and improve economic policy in developing countries. That task in reality should be performed each day of the year by the entire corps of economists that serve the finance ministries, the planning offices, the central

banks, the public investment authorities, and the other
entities of government in each country. Still, certain
very broad conclusions derived from the economic analysis
of the growth process merit some emphasis.

The Relationship between Resources and Earnings

Marginal productivity theory states that under competitive conditions resources tend to be paid an amount
that measures their contribution to total output. This
can be violated under conditions of monopoly or monopsony,
but even under such conditions the difference tends to be
a relatively small percentage. (Monopoly profits consist
of that portion of profits systematically in excess of the
normal or competitive return to capital, as a consequence
of a monopoly enterprise restricting its output below the
competitive level. A firm having monopoly profits equal
to 10 percent of sales is a rarity; one with monopoly profits equal to 20 percent of sales could probably be classified as a miracle. Thus, at most, the marginal product
of purchased inputs might exceed their remuneration by 10
to 20 percent.) The basic proposition, then, is that if a
worker becomes ill, dies, or leaves the country the GDP
will as a consequence be lower than it otherwise would be
by approximately the amount of his or her wage. And when
a capitalist moves his or her wealth to Geneva, the home
country's GDP should suffer (compared to where it otherwise would be) by approximately the gross-rate-of-tax that
the capital would normally earn, times the amount of capital transferred. There is no serious dispute today as to
the relevance of the marginal productivity theory of factor rewards. The issue was met professionally in the
1950s and the early 1960s, and it was shown to apply even
in the agricultural sector of overpopulated India.

There is an extremely deep consequence or implication
of this relationship between resources and earnings. For
it belies totally the idea that there is a thing called
national income, a "pie" as it were, that the government
can somehow decide how to distribute. Quite the contrary.
If a government decides to tax professionals too heavily,
or otherwise reward them too little, many of them will
leave the country. Their contribution to the GDP will at
that point disappear; it will not be left waiting for
others somehow to claim. The same is true for capital.
When capital flees a country, the GDP represented by that
capital's marginal productivity is lost, not transferred
to somebody else. Income--even including, at the end of a

long chain, the interest received on a time deposit--is a
reward for the productivity of resources, not an arbitrary
share of some "pie."

The Importance of Human Capital

It is very clear that attempts to improve the welfare
of large masses of poor people are unlikely to succeed if
such attempts are primarily based on taking money away
from others. The true path of progress in this direction
is increasing the marginal productivity of poor people.
On the whole, all of the principal forces of growth work
in this direction. Adding to a country's stock of physical capital typically increases the marginal productivity
of labor. Technical advances, too, typically increase the
rewards of all or nearly all production factors in a country. But the most important of all sources of increase in
the earnings of workers is the building of human capital.
This process simply converts the same physical entity from
a low-productivity to a high-productivity resource. It
generates the capacity to produce, and therefore to obtain
and enjoy more income. It does this without depriving
anyone else of the capacity to obtain and enjoy income.
All in all, human capital formation is the best prescrip-
tion for the long-term future of those who today are the
poor and needy of the world.

The Recent Record Is Amazingly Good

For the poor people of the world the quarter century
between 1950 and 1975 was probably the best one in history. We should not forget this basic fact. While we in-
quire as to what mistakes were made, as to where we went
wrong, we should also ask ourselves what we did right.
That, in part, was the purpose of the section "Comparing
Successes and Failures," where we compared and contrasted
the behavior of countries in situations of dramatic success and of dramatic failure.

The fact is, of course, that for the great bulk of
human history, generation followed generation with not
much change in anything. Production techniques, levels of
income, the distribution thereof, life expectancy, customs, mores, literacy--all remained approximately constant
from one generation to the next. Probably even the spurts
of civilization that gave rise to the great ancient cul-
tures did not much affect the life of the common man, and
to the extent that they did so, the effect was probably
spread over many centuries.

Consider, then, the record of the recent past. The
World Bank reports that the low-income countries averaged
1.6 percent per year in per capita income growth in the
period since 1960; the middle-income and industrialized
countries averaged 3.7 percent per year. This is a truly
astounding performance. The historic rate of growth of
per capita income in the United States, say from 1900 to
1950, was not much more than 1.5 percent per year. And
this was a period during which the United States was gen-
uinely pulling ahead of most of the rest of the world.
Now, since 1960 we have the poorest of countries doing as
well as the United States did while it was on its way to
reaching its apogee as the dominant economy in the world
(a spot from which it has been clearly receding since
1950).

Moreover, the improvement in welfare as distinct from
income has been even more dramatic. The crude death rate
of the low-income countries today is approximately equal
to that of the middle-income countries in 1960; the crude
death rate of the middle-income countries today, in turn,
is approximately equal to that of the industrialized countries in 1960 (and, indeed, even now, for the latter fig-
ure hasn't changed much). The story with respect to life
expectancy is also impressive. In the low-income countries it went from 42 years in 1960 to 50 years in 1978,
in the middle-income countries from 54 years to 61 years,
and in the industrialized countries from 69 years to 74
years. Thus life expectancy in the low-income countries
is today approximately where it was in the middle-income
countries during the 1950s.

Many factors influenced these dramatic achievements;
surely those related to public health measures and innovations were of great significance. But as far as general
economic growth performance was concerned I again emphasize the human capital aspect. In the low-income countries the proportion of the relevant age group attending
primary school went from 72 to 90 percent for males and
from 37 to 64 percent for females; secondary school attendance went from 14 to 24 percent of their cohort; those in
higher education doubled, from 2 to 4 percent of their cohort. Interestingly, the low-income countries have now
reached levels comparable to those of the middle-income
countries in 1960. It is my hope that by learning from
our successes and our failures and by increasing diligence
in improving the understanding of economic forces and processes of economic science, we can help ensure that this

transformation of the economic lot of the poor of the
world continues for a long time to come.

REFERENCES

Abramovitz, M. 1956. Resources and output trends in the
    United States since 1870. American Economic Review
    46:5-23.
------. 1959. The Allocation of Economic Resources.
    Stanford, Calif.: Stanford University Press.
Balassa, Bela. 1970. Growth strategies in semi-industrial
    countries. Quarterly Journal of Economics 54:1-47.
Bhagwati, Jagdish. 1964. The Economics of Underdeveloped
    Countries. New York: McGraw-Hill.
Denison, E. F. 1962. The Sources of Economic Growth in
    the United States and the Alternatives before Us.
    New York: Committee for Economic Development.
------. 1967. Why Growth Rates Differ: Post-War Exper-
    iences in Nine Western Countries. Washington, D.C.:
    Brookings.
------. 1969. Some major issues in productivity analysis:
    An examination of estimates by Jorgenson and
    Griliches. Survey of Current Business 49 (Pt. 5):1-
    28.
Domar, E. D. 1946. Capital expansion, rate of growth, and
    employment. Econometrica 14:137-47.
------. 1947. Expansion and employment. American
    Economic Review 37:34-55.
------. 1957. Essays in the Theory of Economic Growth.
    New York: Oxford University Press.
Harrod, R. F. 1939. An essay in dynamic theory. Economic
    Journal 49:14-33.
------. 1948. Towards a Dynamic Economics. London:
    Macmillan.
------. 1952. Economic Essays. London: Macmillan.
------. 1963. Themes in dynamic theory. Economic Journal
    73:401-21.
------. 1974. Pure theory of growth economics.
    Zeitschrift fur Nationalokonomie 34:241-47.
Kendrick, J. W. 1961. Productivity Trends in the United
    States. Princeton, N.J.: Princeton University
    Press.
------. 1976. The Formation and Stocks of Total Capital.
    New York: National Bureau of Economic Research.

Krueger, Anne. 1974. The political economy of the rent-
    seeking society. American Economic Review 64 (June):
    291-303.
Kuznets, Simon. 1966. Modern Economic Growth: Rate,
    Structure, and Spread. New Haven, Conn.: Yale
    University Press.
Schultz, Theodore. 1964. Transforming Traditional Agri-
    culture. New Haven, Conn.: Yale University Press.
Solow, R. M. 1956. A contribution to the theory of
    economic growth. Quarterly Journal of Economics 70:
    65-94.
------. 1957. Technical change and the aggregate produc-
    tion function. Review of Economic Statistics 39:312-
    20.
------. 1962. Technical progress, capital formation, and
    economic growth. American Economic Review 52:76-86.
------. 1970. Growth Theory: An Exposition. Oxford,
    Eng.: Clarendon.
World Bank. 1979. World Development Report. New York:
    Oxford University Press.

CONTRIBUTORS

James V. Koch is provost and vice president for academic affairs at Ball State University.

Paul J. Feldstein is professor at the School of Public Health and Department of Economics at the University of Michigan.

Alvin J. Karchere is director of economics at IBM.

Earl O. Heady was director of the Center for Agricultural and Rural Development (CARD) and distinguished professor at Iowa State University.

Robert Dorfman is David A. Wells Professor of Political Economy at Harvard University.

Arnold C. Harberger is distinguished service professor at the University of Chicago.

INDEX

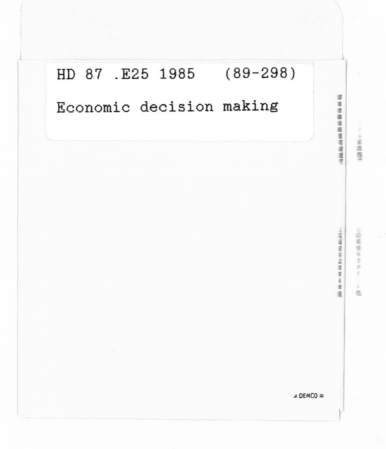